Wake Up...Live the Life You Love,

Giving Gratitude

By
Steven E
&
Lee Beard

Nov 21/06

Doug

Only the best!

Sincerely

Glen Ashmore

Little Seed Publishing, LLC
P.O. Box 4483
Laguna Beach, CA 92652

Pre-Press Management by TAE Marketing Consultations
Robert Valentine, Publications Director;
Lori Powell, Editorial Coordinator;
Rita Robinson, Accounts Manager.

Text and Cover Design: Wm. Gross Magee

Cover Illustrations: Klansee Bell

Publisher intends this material for entertainment and no legal, medical or other professional advice is implied or expressed. If the purchaser cannot abide by this statement, please return the book for a full refund.

Printed in the United States of America

Distributed by Seven Locks Press
3100 W. Warner Ave. #8
Santa Ana, CA 92704

Library of Congress Cataloguing-In-Publication Data
ISBN: 1-933063-01-7

$14.95 USA $24.95 Canada

For your free gift, go to: **www.wakeupand.com**

Other books by Steven E

Wake Up...Live the Life You Love

Wake Up...Live the Life You Love, Second Edition

Wake Up...Shape Up...Live the Life You Love

Wake Up...Live the Life You Love,
Inspirational How-to Stories

Wake Up...Live the Life You Love, In Beauty

Wake Up...Live the Life You Love,
Living on Purpose

Wake Up...Live the Life You Love,
Finding Your Life's Passion

Wake Up...Live the Life You Love,
Purpose, Passion, Abundance

Wake Up...Live the Life You Love,
Finding Personal Freedom

Wake Up...Live the Life You Love,
Seizing Your Success

For your free gift, go to: **www.wakeupand.com**

How would you like to be in the next book with a fabulous group of best-selling authors? Another Wake Up book is coming soon!

Visit: WakeUpLive.com

We would like to provide you with a free gift to enhance this book experience. For your free gift, please visit: WakeUpGift.com

Dedication

To give thanks for the blessings of life is a small thing.

To be able to recognize the blessings is, often, a very large thing, indeed.

To all those who blessed the lives of these authors, we dedicate this book with thanks for your sacrifice, your example, your kindnesses or, simply, for your being. You have changed lives and, now, your influence may enable those of us who write on these pages to help change the lives of others.

Contents

Wake up... Live the Life You Love, Giving Gratitude

Introduction

One of the contributing authors to this volume asked, "What should I write? What is this book about?"

Steven E answered, "Everyone has some reason to be thankful. It probably changed your life. Shouldn't other people know about that?"

And so dozens of writers, speakers, mentors, teachers, entrepreneurs and coaches took up the challenge: find something for which you are grateful and share it with the world. They have accomplished the goal they set for themselves and, in so doing, have already reaped a generous reward of self-knowledge, fond memories, and pure joy.

In these pages you will read of the many reasons each of us has to express gratitude.

You will learn how expressing gratitude will create more reasons to be thankful.

You will even see how you can recognize blessings you might have missed; how you can create your own method of giving thanks, and how these expressions of gratitude will lead to a greater abundance in your life.

Gratitude is very simple, but its effect on our lives can be profound. Turn the page, and begin to feel the power of thankfulness.

Joy to your journey,

Steven E
Lee Beard
2005

When the Downward Slope Looks Long and Steep
Barney King

Not too long ago, I woke up absolutely dreading the possibility of facing another miserable day. You see, a whole series of things hadn't worked out as planned, and when I say that, I mean nothing: nada; zilch. You get the picture. Perhaps you have even been there!

Well, the first task (and really the only task) on my well-considered to-do list was to find the coffee pot and make some serious joe. I did that. My entire meaning in life had been validated in that single act. I was productive. I made coffee; I drank coffee. Everything was looking up.

OK, not quite. I realized that I had already crested; hit the high point of the day. The hill was steep and long and I was looking down.

So what did I do to deserve this? I try hard. I am a nice enough guy. I am really talented. I am smart. My resume looks impressive. But there was no real fulfillment. I wasn't getting anything out of this. THIS was really unfair. Look at all those other successful people in the neighborhood—lots of cars and lots of stuff. In fact, as I surveyed all of THIS, I came to the conclusion that I was a failure. And THIS was the high point of the day!

As I contemplated the sad state of all of THIS, I realized the dog had ever so gently nestled himself on top of my feet. I guess he, the misguided animal that he is, hadn't gotten the message. He seemed to perceive there was some actual value in this resting place on my feet.

Next, my older daughter drove into the kitchen like your basic locomotive, clearing everything out of its path. It seems she overslept and she was late for work. As she threw on her sweater, clutched her purse, grabbed a water bottle and balanced some fruit under her arm, she ran for the door. "Bye Meg, have a great day," I called after her. No response. I looked back at the paper. Next thing I realized, Meaghan is hugging me, saying, "I love you, Dad. Have a great day, too!" Maybe the slope on this hill has changed a bit.

My wife then showed up, also a bit late for work. As she gathered all of her things, she paused and said, "Thanks for the coffee in bed. It always gets my day off to a great start. I really appreciate you for that. You are one special guy." Not quite flat, but the other side of the crest isn't so daunting.

Over the next few minutes, my younger daughter and my son also came through the kitchen, each with their own unique spin on the "You're OK" theme. I finally realized the hill actually had an upslope and I was enthusiastic to find the top.

Viktor Frankl wrote in *Man's Search for Meaning*, the chronicle of his experiences in Nazi concentration camps in Germany, that "everything can be taken from a man but one thing: the last of the human freedoms—to choose one's attitude in any given set of circumstances, to choose one's own way." My family reminded me that day that I had a whole lot to be thankful for. Indeed, the problem wasn't all the things that didn't go right, but rather my attitude.

What goes around comes around. Zig Ziglar expressed it well: "One of the great truths of life is that the more you recognize and express gratitude for the things you have, the more things you will have to express gratitude for."

I re-learned, for seemingly the millionth time, that, first and foremost, we need to look at the world with an attitude of gratitude. We have so much to be grateful for, much that we often take for granted, so much that is truly meaningful—gifts far beyond the things that so often gaudily decorate our lives.

Life is really about love and about relationships. In sharing ourselves, we give love. In giving love, we grow and nourish ourselves, those around us, and the world at large. I got so hung up on the "It's all about me" routine that I failed to consider, acknowledge and appreciate what was really most important in my life: my family and my relationships.

Ꮼ Barney King

Not Ready For Home Yet

Charleen Earley

When we are born, we are given gifts. Not just material ones like pink, blue, or green outfits with cute booties to match, but spiritual ones, too. There are gifts such as kindness, mercy, love, and peace; the list is endless. Sometimes we don't realize that we have certain gifts until someone points them out or we simply begin to use them naturally. I was blessed to be given, among many gifts, the gift of gratitude: That deep down sense of thankfulness for people, animals, events, and even earthly treasures God has placed in my life. I am fortunate to have grown up in one of the most integrated cities in the entire world, Oakland, California. My city included people of many different races, backgrounds, religions, and socio-economic levels. I am thankful to have had the opportunity to absorb and embrace such an array of diversity.

Frequent trips to Fisherman's Wharf and Ghirardelli Square in San Francisco with my mom, older sister, and younger brother were always a pleasure, but this was also a place where we would inevitably see many homeless and hungry souls. It made me sad to see them impoverished, lying on the cold cement with their pets or with their shopping carts filled to the brim with all that they owned. It also gave me a sense of thankfulness that I had a roof over my head, warm clothes to wear, and plenty of food to eat.

As a child, I did not take things for granted. I would always look around and sing songs of praise out loud in the backyard when I thought no one was looking. I'd thank God for the sun, clouds, blades of grass, and my family. I found out later I had an audience after all: my mother. She told me she would watch me through the kitchen window with a smile on her face. I'm sure this gratitude was a gift, not something I had learned.

Our family could be considered middle class. We were not too poor and not too rich. Since I had all my basic needs met, I felt like Goldilocks: life was "just right." We didn't ask our parents for money because we had our lawn-mowing or babysitting jobs. We didn't have separate bedrooms or wall-to-wall carpeting, as some of our friends did. We lived "below the freeway" and went to a high school that did not have funds for certain amenities like a track and football field. For those activities, we were bussed to Brookdale Park. Nevertheless, we still received a decent education. We had a wonderful life!

The first real tragedy of my life occurred when I was 22. I was attacked and beaten by an intruder in my home. My jaw was broken in three places, my left thumb tendon was severed, and my most guarded self was invaded. I witnessed to this man I didn't know throughout the entire assault with the words, "God loves you SO much, you don't have to do this." Even during the most frightening part of the experience, when he held a knife to my chest, I continued to tell him about God's love. Miraculously, my grandma Nani, my angel, came to my rescue and I knew I was safe from any further harm. The man fled and I rushed after him to shut the back door behind him. Bleeding and in shock, I was taken by ambulance to Kaiser Hospital where I recovered physically.

Spiritually, I emerged with a renewed feeling of gratitude for life and for my life's purpose. I knew my work here on earth was not done. I wasn't ready to go home yet. I honestly believe our lives are indestructible, no matter how horrible the accident or tribulation, until God calls us home.

I came out on the other side of that horrifying experience with a new song to share with everyone, this time not in the backyard, but in front of the church congregation. The song was called, "Thank You Lord."

In the years since the attack, my gratitude has continued to multiply. I am thankful for my son, Andrew, and for family members, friends, significant others, and job opportunities. I have a smile that the assailant never stole from me or destroyed.

A gift that sits on a shelf collects dust and has no purpose or meaning. I do my best to use my gift of gratitude daily. If ever discouragement threatens to overtake me, I practice the words of an old Sunday school song, "Count your blessings, name them one by one, count your many blessings, see what God has done!" It always lifts my spirits and puts my life back on purpose with gratitude.

ᢒᴗ Charlene Earley

Everyday Gratitude

Randall Hlavin

"Your happiness in life can best be measured by your everyday expressions of gratitude."

This year I turned fifty-three. For reasons unknown to me, I recently began to reflect on my personal happiness and where I've been and where I'm going in life. This philosophical pondering is not easy to do in our noisy, speedy and sometimes chaotic world—especially in mine. Something deep within told me to take the time, that this is important. As a result, I have realized a spiritual awakening that will carry me forward in life with "everyday gratitude."

This awakening has really captivated me with a promise of a lifetime of happiness. I conclude that there are things that I can and must change to achieve my vision. Only I can define what happiness "looks like," and I must take personal responsibility to get what I want and deserve. I believe to my core, as a human being, that we are meant to live in a state of happiness every day.

Who I am today is the sum of all my fifty-three years on this Earth and the experiences of being with my fellow humans every hour of every day. As I reflect on this thought, I realize that I owed enormous gratitude to many that are still in my life today and those who will be in the future. Who are some of these people?

Without a doubt, my parents head the list. Born in the Depression Era, they have overcome obstacles that are foreign to me. To this day, I still am not able to relate to some of their stories including the now infamous "We had to walk ten miles to school and there was no bus!" They have tried everything they know to do to provide a better life for me, my brother, and sister. Most important are the life lessons on honesty, integrity, hard work, family, and love. These lessons, coupled with my own life experiences, make my parents look smarter by the day! I will be eternally grateful for the brilliant gems of wisdom they gave to me.

I am grateful for my own family. Without them, the wisdom given to me by my parents would have no meaning. They allow me to "practice what I preach" and stretch me beyond belief! Within that stretching lies personal growth and the ability to shape and provide my own brilliant gems of wisdom to the next generation. This is truly a life gift and I am very grateful.

I give thanks for my dearly departed Golden Retriever. How blessed I was to have this animal in my life for fifteen years! From his first days in my arms to his dying before my eyes, he taught me the value of companionship, friendship, and unconditional love. He gave me the ability to deliver this gem of wisdom to anybody who will listen. "We humans should only be so lucky to experience the unconditional love with each other that our pets give to us." I truly loved this dog and am most certainly grateful for his love and lessons he taught me.

There are my educators, business associates, clients, and friends. In your own way, you all tried to teach, mentor, and "just be there" for me. I'm sure I did not always appear grateful—especially when you said "No!" Now, looking back, who has been luckier than I? "No" now means that I am one step closer to "Yes" and I would not have known this without people who cared about me, my goals and dreams. Thank you, each and every one of you. I am humbly grateful.

I have much for which to be grateful and I am filled with gratitude and happiness for the people (and the dog) who helped me get here. Even better, the reflection and these expressions of gratitude have provided me with an insight into personal happiness that heretofore was only an obscure vision.

Looking to my future, this vision is now crystal clear. "Be happy, share happy" is my new motto! My happiness in life will best be measured by my "everyday expressions of gratitude."

ↅ Randall Hlavin

Getting Beyond War One Choice at a Time

Megan Orlando

*T*he ambulance came to the grammar school with sirens blaring. As soon as it stopped, a gurney exploded from the back of the ambulance as two paramedics pushed it toward the school principal who nervously waited to lead them to where 11-year-old Tanesha sat bleeding.

Suffering from a rare genetic neurologic abnormality, Tanesha was free from all pain. Her body was incapable of registering sensations of hot, cold, pressure, pleasure, or pain. She simply had no physical "feelings." To be free of pain was no great blessing. Tanesha sat in the girls' bathroom in a pool of her own blood, her nose obscured beyond recognition, her flesh "picked away" by her own hand. This medical emergency and the family circumstances surrounding her actions brought Tanesha and her family before the Juvenile Court on child abuse and neglect charges.

In the child abuse courts almost everyone is afraid. Parents, children, and relatives are afraid, not knowing what to expect, feeling the extreme seriousness of having children removed from their homes, unsure of what will happen to their family when their case goes to court. Fear, blame, judgment, and punishment were always the rules of engagement in the adversarial process until mediation began to change the way family problems were approached.

Mediation of child abuse and neglect cases is a confidential, neutral process by which a highly-trained mediator, who has no decision-making authority regarding the outcome of the dispute, facilitates communication among the parties. The mediator assists by exploring options and helping the parties reach fully-informed, mutually acceptable solutions that focus on the child's safety and best interests and the safety of all family members.

When Tanesha's parents came to me for mediation they, too, were scared. Neither the mother nor the father thought of themselves as child abusers. They had dreams for their children and worked hard to provide for them. Yet they found themselves separated from their daughter by the court for her own protection.

In mediation each parent told me what they believed to be the problem that caused Tanesha to injure herself. Listening to another person is a gift. When people are allowed to tell their story they experience gratitude. When a person feels that they are being heard, they feel less isolated and that feeling allows gratitude to grow.

Often, when there is conflict, we react rather than listen to each other. Reaction fuels conflict. As a mediator, I have the opportunity to be an observer and to bring my awareness to the situation. I am able to choose my response. I can choose to stay open and listen or I can react. When I experience this freedom, it spreads to those involved in the mediation.

I have learned that when I am able to stay open and hear the story from the other perspective, I meet a part of my own humanity in them. I try to heal the disowned "truth" of the others by listening to all sides. When parents, children, and attorneys have a chance to really hear one another, the ability to make better decisions becomes possible. By answering questions, Tanesha's parents revealed the problem. No one argued or fought. Neither parent had ever hit Tanesha and she desperately wanted to go home. But there was a cold war going on in their home. It was a war of silence. Tanesha's parents had not spoken with each other for five years. To communicate they sent written notes or comments back and forth using their daughter as a messenger. The father worked long hours and the mother worked part time while Tanesha was in school. The silence had grown to be a way of life. This unexpressed conflict was injuring Tanesha, who reflected the dysfunction that was picking away at the family by picking away at her nose until there was little left.

In mediation Tanesha's parents were able to listen to each other and to co-create a family plan. The plan would keep Tanesha safe, keep the family talking, and involve the family in counseling. Tanesha would enter medical behavioral therapy to help her learn about her medical condition and how to protect herself from injury. Fear and silence no longer ruled this family. Eventually, Tanesha was able to return home to a family that was willing to talk through their problems, instead of acting them out.

For me, awareness leads to gratitude. Where there is gratitude we are able to encourage one another to be brave. We can open our hearts and minds, hear the possible, find new choices, learn how to communicate rather than just wanting to "win." We are able to put an end to war.

I am grateful to the parents, children, attorneys, social workers, and judges of the juvenile court for allowing me to facilitate and be a part of their journey to help heal and make whole the lives of families who have become fractured by conflict, pain and the ignorance of not knowing any better. Maya Angelou often says, "When you know better you can do better." The awesome ability of the collective human spirit to grow and move beyond limitations fills me with gratitude. I am thankful for those who can find strength through gratitude to make better choices. Simple choices can create a lifetime of changes, one choice at a time.

ᘓ Megan G. Orlando

Gratitude is Grace

Hazel Palache and Lori Grayson

*G*race: Beauty of form, manner or motion. A pleasing, attractive quality.

We are two women who originate from different worlds, 20 years apart in age.

We come from different nationalities, different religions, and completely different backgrounds. Over the years, we have found that we actually came from the same place—on the inside!

We entered the world authentic and innocent, yet for the majority of our lives, we lived according to others' ideas of how we "should be."

We attempted to be the perfect little girls: pretty, neatly dressed, well behaved, and high achievers. This was the façade we showed to the outside world. Inside we had neither confidence nor self worth. We carried this handicap well into our adult lives.

We discovered that as young women, we had both paid lip service to gratitude. We said how lucky we were to have what we had because that's what we were supposed to do. In actuality we took everything for granted. We assumed that everyone had at least what we had or better. Perhaps we felt that we were entitled to the good things in life to make up for the things we didn't have, like self-acceptance. During our early years, gratitude was really just a word in the dictionary.

As our lives unfolded, we took similar paths: college, work, marriage, kids. We lived upper middle class lives lacking nothing material. We had all the trappings of success and happiness. From the outside nothing had changed, our lives still appeared "perfect." However, we were having different internal conversations. We lived our lives going through the motions, thinking that we really should be happy and fulfilled. Inside we focused on what might go wrong, what we didn't have, and how we might fail and we often got caught in spirals of fear and despair!

Our illusions of perfection were finally shattered as our marriages dissolved and we found it was time to get 'real' and reclaim our authenticity. Although the actual catalyst was different for each of us, our journeys paralleled as we found our way back. Learning to experience true gratitude was integral to the growth we experienced as our lives unfolded. It played a major role in improving our attitudes. We learned from our experiences and those of others in a completely different manner. As we worked with the tools and discoveries we made, our lives changed.

We began to work with our own energy and make positive differences. And we became more and more grateful! To this day, giving thanks and having gratitude continues to provide us with the energy to overcome obstacles.

We have worked with thousands of clients in our practices and found that the majority of people suffer from the same issues that we have experienced. They were out of touch with themselves. Gratitude became a cornerstone as we taught them to create their own power and success in life. We asked our clients to look at what they did have and at the wonder of who they were, instead of what they didn't have and who they weren't. We taught people that perfectionism is "crazy making." We were happy to share the lessons we had learned.

We've focused on the negatives and we've focused on the positives. Our not-so-surprising conclusion is that focusing on what we want is, without doubt, the winner! It creates a more positive, successful life. We're not saying that the journey has been easy; it was actually rather bumpy for both of us. However, once we made up our minds to make the changes, it was really quite simple and the rewards have been immeasurable.

Look at the wonderful, simple things in life to be grateful for. Hot running water, indoor plumbing, good food, and telephones are incredible luxuries. We have the freedom and ability to work, to love, to laugh, and to play. More often than not, people take these gifts for granted. When we forgo the negatives and look at the blessings all around us, even drudgery can become magical.

We all have choices. Choose your environment and friends wisely. Choose to do the things that you love to do. Don't let anyone steal your dreams. Listen carefully to what people say, that's the way they really think. Negative people really are energy drains and there are many people who get fulfillment from staying stuck. Even in positive

Wake up... Live the Life You Love, Giving Gratitude

situations they will tend to find the negative. The past has already happened and you don't know exactly what the future will bring. It's all about now.

We believe that everything that happens is, in some way, a blessing provided so that we may learn a lesson. We're very grateful for every experience we've had. These experiences have allowed us to become the women we are today, doing the work we love, finding an unusual friendship, and being grateful for each day. We suggest that you use some of the same simple tools. Watch how things change—you'll be amazed! Here are four steps to help you get started:

- Start a gratitude journal
- Write daily affirmations
- Learn to Master the way you think
- Be of Service to others

We continue to experience grace everyday through being truly grateful for everything in life. We wish you success on your journey.

ℰℴ Hazel Palache and Lori Grayson

Wake up... Live the Life You Love, Giving Gratitude

Great Lessons Begin Early

Greg Reid

*L*et me share a quick story about how a simple childhood conversation made an impact on the life I lead today.

During a recent radio interview, the host asked where I came up with the lessons I shared in my latest book, *Positive Impact*. My response surprised even me as I recalled the answer. You see, I was very fortunate to have grown up with a wonderful role model. Even when I was a child, my mother spoke to me on a mature level, taught me lessons that have lasted and have impacted the lives of many people within my circle.

For example, I share a lesson in *Positive Impact* that came from a car ride when I was about 12 years old. My mom was telling a story about something that had happened at her workplace when I piped in and said something along the lines of, "I would never do that if that was me." An eerie silence filled the car. It was an uncomfortable moment, and then my mom turned toward me and said these words: "Pop quiz. Say you have some very important people coming into your business to close a major deal with you and your organization. Now, the place is a mess because the cleaning people never showed up and the office and bathroom need a major overhaul. Quick! What would you do? Would you: Call the janitor's office and yell at them for not doing their job? Would you change the meeting place because the office is just too messy to deal with? Or would you clean it yourself?"

My response was short and simple: "I'd change the location AND yell at the cleaning crew. After all, I'm the boss, right? Cleaning toilets is NOT my job!"

My Mom turned toward me and lowered her head with a look of disappointment, shaking it from side to side as she responded in a quiet tone, "That's a shame. You'll never be a leader then."

"What?" I belted. "You said I already WAS the leader. You said I was the boss."

"No," she whispered. "As a leader, you would be willing to do anything and everything necessary to create success for yourself and others, no matter what, even if it meant cleaning an office. Real

Wake up... Live the Life You Love, Giving Gratitude

leaders are willing to chip in and help in any circumstance. Funny thing," she continued. "If you were that kind of a leader, it's likely you would never have to worry about situations like this because others would want to help you look good."

Even at that young age, I remember having one of those "Aha" moments when things seem so clear.

In my adult years, I remember staying at work after hours one day to clean up a bit and do a little wall painting. A couple of employees came up behind me and asked, "Why are you doing that? Shouldn't you hire someone to do that stuff?" Suddenly, the student became the teacher as I shared the same story with them that my mom had shared with me. Hours went by as they stayed behind to help me deck out the office that night, never asking for a thing in return. One of those people became his own boss, and now has a company of his own. I often wonder how many people he's told this story to, along with the other great advice my mom shared with me over the years.

Well, Mom, for myself and the others whom your wisdom has affected, I want to say, "thank you," I love you, and whatever you do, Keep Smilin'!

                                 ☙ Gregory Scott Reid

The Gift of Struggle

Isabelle Tierney

As a holistic therapist, I am always struck by the amount of shame and self-loathing experienced by those of us who struggle with addiction. Though many of us lead apparently full lives, our inability to "conquer" what is perceived as a controllable issue impacts even the most joy-filled moments. Entrenched in the belief that happiness will be ours as soon as we achieve self-control, we torture ourselves with harsh recriminations and self-inflicted emotional isolation, missing the beauty that lies all around us.

What if we were taught that our "struggle" with addiction is in fact just as Divine as anything else? What if we could understand that it is a powerful way into Peace and Love? Could we find gratitude in it then?

I spent most of my life trying to attain happiness by striving to get over my addiction to food. I really thought that I would be happy the day my struggle disappeared. I read countless stories of people who had conquered their weight and who now lived a supposedly perfect and blissful life. I so wanted to believe that, I too, could be a new person if only I could stop overeating; A person without any fears or faults; A person without suffering. It all seemed so easy.

For twenty-five years, I did everything I could to try to be healed of my eating disorder: I exercised like an Olympic athlete, ate reduced-calorie meals and snacks and gave myself a good tongue lashing when I failed at either. Unfortunately, I was not getting rid of my struggle; in fact, it was getting worse. The more I tried to conquer my addiction, the stronger it came at me. I kept right on going, though, for I knew it had to be my fault, my lack of willpower or self-control. I always resolved to be better the next day, and I would start the whole vicious cycle all over again.

As the years passed though, I started noticing something strange. Living with and working on my eating disorder was actually bringing forth gifts that were enriching other aspects of my life. Every good quality I developed through my "struggle" became a quality that showed up in my parenting, my healership, my wifehood, and my friendships. The process of dealing with my eating disorder taught me to become more patient, compassionate, and loving. It allowed me to see the sacredness of our world and to feel gratitude for every moment. It helped me curb my impulsivity, soften my criticism and judgments, curb my tendency to objectify, and let go of my self-centeredness. As the effects of these internal changes began to ripple outward to all my relationships, I found that a deeper, more lasting happiness began to creep in.

I started seeing that my addiction connected me to parts of my being that were usually hidden. I had a tendency to live in my mind, lost in a world of thought where I felt safe. I did not want to drop into my feelings, my body, or any places that were unknown. My binges and purges invited me to leave the world of the mind and enter foreign territory. I expected to find suffering, terror, and pain. What I found instead was revolutionary: Everything is the Beloved. Sadness, hate, love, and even judgments are the Beloved. Pain is the Beloved. Joy is the Beloved. Addiction is the Beloved. I am the Beloved.

Today, I no longer see my addiction as something I need to get rid of. Doing so never really worked for long anyway. It only froze my perception of having inner enemies I needed to vanquish, which kept me in a perpetually tight and angry state. This gave my addiction fertile ground from which to grow. Instead, I stay present with life's manifestations as they arise and welcome them all as the sacred energies that they are. My compulsion to overeat has dramatically lessened. I feel tremendous gratitude, inordinate joy, and awe at the creativity that I get to live every moment of every day. The struggle is over. Won't you join me?

ᴄ⁄ᴈ Isabelle Tierney

Minding Your Mind In The Moment With Gratitude!
Diane Ulicsni, CHT

*T*he attitude of Gratefulness holds the power to heal! Gratitude has the power to instantly change your life. This potent inner mechanism brought me from despair, helplessness and trauma to joy, love and living my dreams!

My childhood years were full of loneliness; of feeling unwanted and unloved. When I was 18 months old I had measles that settled in my eyes, as a result I had crossed eyes. Because of my eyes, people wouldn't look at me and treated me as if I was retarded. Most people tried to avoid me—even my own family. After a long illness, my mother died when I was nine. My father couldn't handle this loss. He escaped into alcohol and rage then abandoned me and my sister.

After my mother's death I lived from home to home. When I was 14, a relative asked me to move in with her. She needed help with her seven children. We lived in a two-room house and we were dirt poor. I decided I had to be the "good girl" so I would have a place to live. I cooked, cleaned, and did whatever I could to be needed so they wouldn't throw me out.

High school was extremely painful. Because of my crossed eyes I had a very hard time seeing. I tried to smile a lot, but I was still an outcast. I was so full of loneliness and pain. I often prayed to just stop feeling.

I left my small town in northern Minnesota for the Twin Cities the day after I graduated high school. I remember being full of hope and optimistic that I was going to be somebody. When I was 20, I was able to pay for surgery to fix my eyes. Although I was glad to have my eyes fixed I still had emotional problems to deal with.

Very soon after high school, I started developing panic attacks. At that time, nobody seemed to know what panic attacks were. Doctors thought I was faking. I felt I was going crazy. My anxiety and panic attacks got steadily worse as the years went by. I tried counseling, but got no relief. I was desperate, deeply depressed and I wondered whether I could go on.

One day I saw an ad for a self-hypnosis course. I was nervous about taking the class, but I was desperate. I soon found that I could control my panic and anxiety. The more I practiced the new skills that I had learned, the more relief I felt. I began to have more energy and enthusiasm. I sought out books, classes, and any training I could find on hypnosis. My life improved tenfold! I studied NLP and trauma therapy so I could continue my own healing and then be able to share with others what I have learned.

It is now over 30 years later, and I seldom have anxiety. The panic attacks have stopped completely. I am so very grateful that my panic and anxiety drove me to seek out every avenue to resolve my problems. I found and developed solutions that worked and quickly discarded those that didn't. Because of my anxiety I became a successful therapist and coach. I learned that healing was possible and then was compelled to help others. I now specialize in finding fast and efficient solutions for people with a multitude of problems. Today I am living my dream. I create hypnosis and guided imagery programs and try to help as many people as possible be able to feel and live as well as I do.

The inner experience of gratitude changed my physiology and my mind set. I remember feeling so grateful each time I got relief from my symptoms. Holding an attitude of gratitude with each improvement empowered me to keep going and create a life of joy and fulfillment.

I am grateful for the sixth grade teacher, Mr. Lucas who encouraged me to sing. He saw the potential in me and wouldn't let me quit. He told me I had a beautiful voice and that they missed me when I wasn't at school. Because of his words and because he would look right at me, I kept showing up. Mr. Lucas showed me that one person with a few chosen words of love and encouragement can change a life.

Most of all I am grateful for a life that has taught me so much and has put me in a position to help transform the lives of others.

If you want to change your life, stop and consider what you are grateful for. In every moment and every circumstance you can find something to be grateful for. Gratitude will change your thoughts and feelings, your behavior and actions. If you always look for a reason to be grateful, your life will be transformed in a powerful way.

I am grateful for my childhood - it taught me to be self-reliant and always to have hope!

I am grateful that I had crossed eyes as a child, because my experiences taught me how important it is to look beyond the surface and find the inner person. I am grateful for the panic attacks, because they caused me to find tools, techniques, and inner resources that I never knew existed.

I am grateful for this opportunity to share this with you!

ᘓ Diane Ulicsni

Even a Safety Pin

Erin Snyder-Dixon

*I*cy air bit at our fingers. Breezy spikes poked randomly through layers of fabric. Whirls of cold air snaked up around our ankles and mixed with hard earned perspiration. Cold and wet—the double whammy of training anti-comfort. We were training for a 60 mile walk to raise funds and awareness, in hopes of stomping out breast cancer.

One foot in front of the other. We kept pushing forward, trusting that we could finish; trusting that we could make a difference. Pushing just a little bit closer to being truly grateful for the trust, with a lesson in Gratitude.

The weather had changed without warning and the temperature continued to drop as the wind gained resolve. We were unprepared for the change. June's jacket had lost the single button that had once married the two sides of the lapel, giving the cold air a free pass at her upper body.

"Do you have a safety pin?" June asked. I fumbled in my fanny pack. I had bandages, a pedometer and cell phone—but; no safety pin. I checked my pockets, and, again, came up empty.

"Sorry. You want to head back?" I asked. I already knew the answer, but I had to ask at least.

"If only I had a safety pin," she said, obviously annoyed at the thought of cutting short a training walk. June wrapped her arms tightly around her waist to secure her jacket, and on we went.

We saw it at the same time. There, on the sidewalk, was a shaped and looped piece of stainless steel. A perfect safety pin!

We said it at the same time. "Even a safety pin." We were so grateful for the tiny piece of twisted metal. Once again, our need had been met. It wasn't the first time and it won't be the last. It did, however, leave an imprint and reinforced what we already knew. God would take care of our need. Singular, one at a time. Sometimes, before we knew we needed it and sometimes, only after we asked. Our Creator had found yet another way to prove the He really is in the details! Our training walk would go on.

Wake up... Live the Life You Love, Giving Gratitude

There was a need, there was the asking, and there was the receiving. That safety pin has become a symbol and reminder that we can trust. Trust, that our Creator hears even the smallest and quietest prayer. Trust, that if it is part of His plan, it will be provided. We might have to ask, and we might have to work hard to lay the groundwork. Hard work still matters. Planning still counts. And, in an imperfect world, bad things still happen.

"Even a safety pin" has become our way of saying, "He did it again." Sometimes all you have to do, is ask. Get out of your own way, and stop tripping over your pride. When you get to the point where you can let go and trust, you become grateful for the comfort of trust, not what you receive. Trust is getting out of the driver's seat and putting faith in a Higher Power.

We found our "Safety pin" just when we needed it. Our training walk went on. We finished our fundraising and made a difference. But the biggest impact was on us. Our literal find has become a figurative symbol. A symbol of trust and gratitude. A symbol of our Creator's ability to show promise in even a small piece of twisted metal. Don't get me wrong; we have lots of symbols. If we open our eyes and see, we have so much to be grateful for.

True gratitude leaves more than a thank you. It leaves an imprint. It changes you, it changes others- if you let it.

The proof is all around you—if you need it. Look for it, find it, believe it, and be grateful for it. I'll bet you have many stories of Gratitude for all of life's "safety pins."

ↄ Erin Snyder-Dixon

Wake up... Live the Life You Love, Giving Gratitude

Embrace Silence

Dr. Wayne Dyer

You live in a noisy world, constantly bombarded with loud music, sirens, construction equipment, jet airplanes, rumbling trucks, leaf blowers, lawn mowers and tree cutters. These manmade, unnatural sounds invade your sense and keep silence at bay.

In fact, you've been raised in a culture that not only eschews silence, but is terrified of it. The car radio must always be on, and any pause in conversation is a moment of embarrassment that most people quickly fill with chatter. For many, being alone in silence is pure torture.

The famous scientist Blaise Pascal observed, "All man's miseries derive from not being able to sit quietly in a room alone."

With practice, you can become aware that there's a momentary silence in the space between your thoughts. In this silent space, you'll find the peace that you crave in your daily life. You'll never know that peace if you have no spaces between your thoughts.

The average person is said to have 60,000 separate thoughts daily. With so many thoughts, there are almost no gaps. If you could reduce that number by half, you would open up an entire world of possibilities for yourself. For it is when you merge in the silence, and become one with it, that you reconnect to your source and know the peacefulness that some call God. It is stated beautifully in Psalms, "Be still and know that I am God." The key words are "still" and "know."

"Still" actually means "silence." Mother Teresa described the silence and its relationship to God by saying, "God is the friend of Silence. See how nature (trees, grass) grows in silence; see the stars, the moon and the sun—how they move in silence. We need silence to be able to touch souls." This includes your soul.

It's really the space between the notes that makes the music you enjoy so much. Without the spaces, all you would have is one continuous, noisy note. Everything that's created comes out of silence. Your thoughts emerge from the nothingness of silence. Your words come out of this void. Your very essence emerged from emptiness.

All creativity requires some stillness. Your sense of inner peace depends on spending some of your life energy in silence to recharge your batteries, remove tension and anxiety, thus reacquainting you with the joy of knowing God and feeling closer to all of humanity. Silence reduces fatigue and allows you to experience your own creative juices.

The second word in the Old Testament observation, "know," refers to making your personal and conscious contact with God. To know God is to banish doubt and become independent of others' definitions and descriptions of God. Instead, you have your own personal knowing. And, as Meville reminded us so poignantly, "God's one and only voice is silence."

c/s Dr. Wayne Dyer

Thousands Have This Priceless Gift – But Rarely Give It
Beth Carls and Amy Looper

*E*ach of us is an influencer, someone who influences others. With every thought, word, or deed, we are constantly influencing the world around us. American writer William Channing says, "Others are affected by what I am and say and do. And these others also affect others. So a single act of mine may spread in widening circles through a nation of humanity."

For some of us, the influence of our school teachers has given us hope and motivation, and has contributed greatly to our successes. We are grateful for their positive influence and have learned that expressing gratitude is important, not just for us, but for those around us. Studies show that over 50% of our nations' teachers feel hopeless. That is both sad and shocking. But can you imagine how quickly that statistic could be reduced if we simply take the time to show our gratitude—to say "thank you" to those who have helped change our lives? As Channing points out, "that simple action could ripple out and create a meaningful moment for teachers and for our own children as they model our behavior and show gratitude to the teachers who have most influenced them in a positive way."

Recently, we made a decision to start doing a better job of showing gratitude to our teachers, especially in light of the fact that so many teachers are struggling with hopelessness. Here's how we came to our decision: In the summer of 2005, our company, MindOH!, had the honor of participating in the Houston A+ Externship Program. This model program connects classroom teachers with business professionals. The idea is to help make students' learning experiences more relevant to the workplace. A teacher extern is assigned to work with a business for one week so that an exchange of ideas can occur. This can help educators gain a better understanding of the business world.

The extern Pat was assigned to work with us. Pat was excited about how our educational programs improve relationships among kids, parents, and educators, and also help increase academic learning and reduce the power struggle in typical adult-child interactions in homes and schools across the country. When her week with us ended, she felt grateful for our time, our dedication to her profession, and our efforts to make her feel a part of the MindOH! team. But it was her gift of wisdom that had such a powerful influence over us.

Throughout our week together, Pat showed us how our worlds—business and education—are really not that much different and how we can better help one another address the needs of teachers and students. Here are two examples:

Management By Walking Around (MBWA) was shared as the one thing top-notch school administrators need to learn. By walking around their campuses, administrators have the opportunity to show something that is so easy to give, yet so rarely given—gratitude. MBWA gives them the opportunity to express their gratitude for all the things that teachers do each day to teach our children. Just showing up helps teachers feel valued and validated.

Lifelong Learning was another important lesson we learned from our extern.

What Pat said, what she did and who she was had such a great influence on us. She modeled the importance of lifelong learning. Although she had spent all but the last five years of her career as a fine arts teacher, she enthusiastically embraced the opportunity to learn a variety of new digital media. And she did it with such gusto! We, on the other hand, had the opportunity to observe her flexibility to adapt and change, something many of us in the business world spend a lot of time trying to figure out, and something MindOH! wants to teach students.

Our experience with Pat reminded us of all the wonderful gifts that teachers bring to our students each day. How sad it is to consider that there are teachers, like Pat, sitting in classrooms each day feeling unappreciated, underpaid, and hopeless.

As a result of our experience with Pat, we're committed to showing more gratitude to the teachers who have made such a difference in our lives. We want to help others do so too, by giving them the opportunity to show their gratitude to a favorite teacher. In other words, we want to widen the circle of gratitude for all the important work that classroom teachers do each day. What about you? Do you have a gratitude story to tell? Would you send us your story of the teacher or teachers who had the biggest impact on you? We would love to hear from you.

✐ Beth Carls and Amy Looper

For your free gift, go to: **www.wakeupand.com**

Only Love

Melissa Gokmogol-Broussard
Dedicated to my mom and my late father

*L*ike many teenagers, I used to think that I could not stand my parents. After all, I knew better. What did they know about life? That was my way of thinking even long after my teenage years. I resented any input, any suggestion they might have had about my life, or life in general. I came to the United States to attend college, then got married and stayed.

After 5 years, I found myself going through a divorce. I talked to my parents, and they suggested that they move here and provide emotional support for me during my divorce. Since my Dad was retired at the time, nothing was holding them back in my home country. Without hesitation my parents moved across the globe and came to the United States.

You are probably thinking "how sweet" or "how wonderful." Well, at first it sounded like a great idea, but once they were here, expressing their opinions and ideas about my life, I went back to being a teenager: I resented them. They had sacrificed their nice comfortable life to come to a place where they couldn't even understand the language, and I was resenting their input into my life. A couple of years after their arrival, I realized the sacrifice they had made and I came to the conclusion that they truly loved me. Wasn't that a novel idea? Since my parents were not the sort to hug and kiss me all the time, I had always thought "they don't love me." After that realization, I saw my parents in a totally different way. They were not annoying anymore and I did not resent their input. "Aha!" I finally started enjoying my parents' company.

After they had lived here for 12 years my parents decided to go back home. That was in 2003. They moved back home in March and I called my Dad on Father's Day in June. He was so happy to hear from me. We spoke for a little while and before we hung up I said, "I love you Dad." On June 29th, my father passed away. That had been my last conversation with him. I am so glad that, in the last interaction I had with my Dad, I told him that I loved him and was able to really feel it and mean it.

I am very grateful for the intimate time I was able to spend with my parents. I am so grateful that they supported me in every way possible. Most important, I am so glad that my last words to my Dad were "I love you." If, ten years earlier, I had not realized how much my parents loved me, my last conversation with my Dad would probably have been very different. I would have missed ten wonderful years of closeness with my parents. The intimate times we miss with our loved ones can never be regained. Be grateful for being alive, for being with your loved ones and for the love you have for each other.

When we put everything else aside, what is left?

Only love.

∽ Melissa Gokmogol-Broussard

The Universe Does Not Operate On a "Three Strikes Law"
Sarah Chloe Burns

*T*hank heavens! Consider the myriad and multitudinous implications of a universal "three strikes, you're out" rule. Does this rule exist? Should this rule exist? If we take a look at history, we find, we are given the capability to forgive as well as the joy in being forgiven.

If we are to believe the Old Testament, the answer is revealed to us through God's actions. God was so disappointed in Adam and Eve's transgression in Eden that He removed innocence from humankind forever—replacing it with original sin. Later, God's remorse deepened; He repented that He had ever created humanity and sent a flood upon the earth to destroy all but His righteous servant, Noah (and his family, by default). Following the flood, He was saddened by the destruction and sent the rainbow as His assurance He would never again destroy the earth. In Abraham's day, the Lord's righteous indignation drove Him to swear upon the destruction of all of Sodom and Gomorrah. With Abraham's pleadings, however, God was coerced into sparing any righteous persons within this sinful region (i.e., his nephew Lot and his family — once again, by default).

Well, there you have it—four regrets from the Creator Himself. Must we judge Him eternally? Centuries later, enlightenment inquiry would drive honest and devout men to challenge Church authority that was based upon both Old and New Testament "rules."

During the Age of Enlightenment, Copernicus (not merely a mathematician and astronomer, but a clergyman as well) began to turn the spiritual world upside down with his observations in, *On The Revolutions of the Heavenly Spheres* (1543). Challenging the ancient Aristotelian and church theory (based on Biblical passages) that the earth was the center of the universe, and that the sun "rose and sat" in rotation about the earth, Nicolaus Copernicus observed planetary rotations and declared ours a solar-centered system. He escaped papal denunciation by publishing his findings at the end of his life.

Later, the famed starry dreamer, Galileo Galilei, improved upon a Flemish invention called the telescope and was able to confirm the Copernican theory. One of the Inquisitors, Cardinal Bellarmine, soundly warned Galileo that the consensus of the Holy Fathers must be observed, according to the Council of Trent. Both Old and New Testament scriptures implied that the earth was the center of the universe. If those verses could so easily be set aside, how far might the new science go toward removing Biblical and papal authority altogether? Galileo was censored and exiled for his honesty—not unlike his mutually risk-taking predecessor from Galilee.

Christ used symbolism and parable in order to impart deep spiritual lessons to those who hungered for true righteousness; he also intended to bypass the religious scholars of his day, in order to spread his wisdom as long as possible ("These things are hidden from the wise and prudent"). Therefore, the precision of his words must be weighed against the lesson he was striving to impart. He was neither a mathematician nor a scientist, but it is certain he never intended his message to be a validation for inquisition and execution. In fact, his brand of spirituality can best be seen in the *actual and scientific* laws of the universe.

Newton's third law established the "principle of mutual gravitation." That is, for every action, there is an equal and opposite reaction. Is there a spiritual lesson here? Most certainly, and it agrees with both the eastern law of karma, and Christ's admonition to cast your bread upon the waters, and after many days it will return to you.

Every action we take has a consequence (now that is scary). The universe *does* have a perfect accounting system, and we must play our part in balancing the books. Fortunate to our survival, we may go deep into debt, but we also have the opportunity to draw upon the great reserves God has created to forgive and cover our transgressions. Our eventual destiny, however, is to transcend our karma (in Christianity, that means forgive others so that we may likewise be forgiven). Thereby, our debts can be transmuted as we climb the mountain.

Happily, I like to compare this system of salvation to my favorite sport—tennis. I can lose hundreds of points in a row, be down one set and love-five in the second (one more game and the match is lost), and still manage to retrieve victory from the jaws of defeat.

Universal law works the same. The "three strikes, you're out" rule does not apply in our life game. As long as the game is afoot, we can come out winners. Thank God! Otherwise, heaven would be a very lonely paradise.

ᴄᴠ Sarah Chloe Burns

The Little Things
Scott Kudia, Ph.D

Think back to when your relationship was brand new. Do you recall how everything he or she did was exciting, cute, endearing, or brilliant? Remember how fun everything was and how perfect your new love seemed to be? The relationship was easy. He could do no wrong. Then one day he said or did something that didn't sit right with you and you thought, "Uh-oh." Soon that odd little behavior was one big annoying habit that caused you to end the relationship. Where did it go wrong? He was so amazing. She was so perfect. What happened?

In the beginning little imperfections are ignored as we focus on the things we love about our new mate. Over time, though, our focus shifts and the little imperfections become magnified while the things we love are disregarded. Soon those little quirks become intolerable habits and we break it off. Then what happens? We miss him. We forget about those annoying habits and focus once again on all the little things we love so much about him. We miss her great laugh or his experimental cooking or how nice it is to cuddle together in front of the television. Instead of getting over him we wonder how to get him back.

The best way to love someone is to be grateful for his love. When you're grateful for his love you behave differently toward him. Instead of resentment you convey respect. Rather than annoyed you feel amused. You choose loving over loathing. When you respond differently to him he responds differently toward you. Remember, little things can either strengthen or weaken the relationship. Therefore, you decide what kind of relationship it will be by which of the little things you focus on.

Water can take the form of solid, liquid, or gas. It doesn't matter if it's ice, liquid, or steam—it's still water. Relationships respond the same way. Whether it is love, indifferent, estranged, flowing, stuck, or invisible, a relationship exists. When it is stuck and cold like ice we have conflict and resentment. When it's invisible like gas we are indifferent to our partner and don't remember why we're in the relationship to begin with. When it's flowing like liquid it's exciting and fulfilling. In order to keep the relationship flowing we must remind ourselves how grateful we are for the love we have. We must express love and gratitude every day for those little things that made us choose our partner in the first place.

When we think of a loved one it isn't the great body or the nice car or the fat bank account that makes us feel warm inside. It's the way he says your name. It's her warm, compassionate eyes or his smile that makes you melt. It's the way he makes you laugh or the way she nurtured you when you were sick. It's driving three hours each way just to see her on weekends or how he surprised you by laughing when you spilled strawberry pie all over his car rug. It's the way you feel safe in his arms. These are the things we remember. When your life flashes before your eyes I guarantee you won't remember him leaving the toilet seat up or not loading the dishwasher the "right" way.

When we're grateful for the little things we love we realize the annoying things don't really matter. When we focus too much on what annoys us, (and we all do from time to time), we need to step back and remember what we love about our mate. Take a moment to make a list of everything you love about your partner. Then share it with him or her. Keep the list with you and pull it out the next time he leaves his dirty underwear on the floor. Review the list whenever she spends too much time getting ready. Remind yourself what it is about your partner you are grateful for. Our irritations come from a perceived refusal to conform to the way we think things should be. These perceptions are all in our head. Gratitude comes from the heart. When you come from a place of gratitude everything else becomes inconsequential. There is only love.

✑ Scott Kudia, Ph.D

A Couple's Last Goodbye

Steven Fisher and Terry Morganti-Fisher

On a Thursday night a few months before my wife and I were to be married, we received a call inviting us to a ceremony honoring our friend Robert. He was too ill to attend.

Less than a year before, he had been diagnosed with terminal cancer. He had tried everything, including traditional and holistic treatments, but now he had been sent home under Hospice care to die with dignity and honor in the presence of his family and loved ones. His last few hours were coming, but nobody knew exactly when.

With each mile that passed, we decided that we wanted to see Robert, but word had already gone out that he wasn't accepting visitors. Following an impulse, we called his wife to see if Robert might like us to perform Reiki on him. We had heard that this hands-on treatment was one thing that brought him peace and relief. His wife confirmed that our instincts were correct. She gratefully invited us to come.

When we arrived, one of the neighbors was standing guard, making Fort Knox security look tame. She'd known us for years, but she was <u>not</u> going to let us in until she got permission from upstairs. Even then, she warned us that Robert looked "very different." We assured her that we were stalwart enough souls to be in his presence, and we ascended to the master bedroom.

When we entered, Robert's wife made room for us at his side. Robert didn't have much muscular control, and he was having trouble breathing, so he had to stay propped up in a half-sitting position. His breathing was shallow, but it wasn't labored or wheezing. His wife was feeding him ice chips with a spoon, and he looked at her with appreciative eyes while we positioned ourselves at his side and feet.

There were a lot of things that Robert could no longer do. Sometimes he bit the spoon without knowing when he tried to eat his ice. His head wandered around, barely under control.

But there were a few things that Robert <u>could</u> do. He had a radiant smile and seemed to be experiencing some incredible loving gratitude, particularly at moments when he was lucid enough to realize that he was with his wife of almost twenty years, as she held him and stroked his hair. It was a beautiful lesson in love to see how these two people could still express such love and affection for one another. Sometimes Robert would fix his gaze on us with such intensity that we wondered what he saw. Was he just intrigued with the experience of looking at us? Could he see love in us, or angels? Did he see God? We had no way of knowing.

Robert's spiritual leader read from their holy texts, and soft inspirational music played in the background. At times all of us would start singing along quietly, as if on cue. We all seemed to be tuned in to a higher power. We glanced at each other from time to time, acknowledging without words that this was where we were supposed to be. Finally, Robert dozed off for awhile and his wife managed to take a much needed nap. It would be the last time they would sleep in the same room together, at least in their physical bodies.

Robert's daughter came in a short while later, waking them up. We noticed that his energy had changed. His slumping was worse, so we lifted and propped him back up with pillows, as best we could. His breathing more shallow now. We heard those first whispers of wheeziness and sensed that it would be over soon. We went to get his other daughter, who had already gone to bed. She asked if her daddy wanted to see her. We didn't know what to say to this sweet 11-year-old whose father was about to depart, but looking back, we believe it was exactly what Robert would have asked for, if he could have spoken.

Robert's wife climbed into bed behind him and wrapped her arms around him. His daughters were on each side, and we moved down by his feet. Other relatives gathered around. Just as Robert breathed his last, the phone rang. It was Robert's mother-in-law calling. Somehow, mothers just know these things. The room was softened by a peaceful, loving reverberation. We could feel the sacredness of the moment.

This experience was a profound gift to us as we prepared to enter into our own marriage and we thank Robert and his wife for sharing it with us. We acknowledge that we both received something precious, being able to witness this loving couple saying good-bye. To this day, it reminds us of how short our time is together, and that we each have a choice: We can get caught up in our busy lives, neglecting each other and taking our relationships for granted, or we can be grateful for each and every hour we have together. Gratitude is a choice, and we choose to spend our days wisely and well, for we know each day together is just too precious to waste.

ᗡ Steven Fisher and Terry Morganti-Fisher

Wake up... Live the Life You Love, Giving Gratitude

Thankful for *Us and Our Children*
Twila Prindle

*C*an you imagine creating a generation of successful young entrepreneurs that are changing the face of the world? Can you imagine working hand in hand with the next generation of millionaires some of whom are as young as 6 years old?

I have so much to be thankful for. Everyday I work with the kids at *Us And Our Children, Inc.* I am thankful that they allow me to truly live the life I love. I founded *Us And Our Children, Inc.,* about two years ago, teaching children financial literacy and independence through entrepreneurship. After having been homeless, hungry, unemployed, and broke, I decided that I didn't want anyone else to experience the heartache that came with these deprivations. After much prayer and meditation it became very clear to me what I needed to do. When I made that decision, God placed person after person in my path to aid me in taking my program and my kids to another level.

I am so thankful to have been mentored by Gregory Scott Reid who showed me how to turn my passion into payday. I am grateful to Cappi Pidwell, who helped me find a deeper inner peace through meditation. I am thankful for Bret Treadwell, who introduced me to Pastor Clinton Bush. Pastor Bush has truly mentored me and my children with his love, excitement, motivation, and commitment to success. I cannot close without giving the kids at *Us and Our Children* a shout out of thanks for all of their hard work! They created flip flops, greeting cards, janitorial businesses, books, CDs, coloring books, bake stands, and the list goes on and on. I am so proud and so very thankful for them.

Because of them, I am already thankful for the future.

ᴄ⋙ Twila Prindle

Wake up... Live the Life You Love, Giving Gratitude

Does This Sound Familiar?

Michelle Quay

I made good money, I came from a good family. I did not have one of those intriguing rags to riches stories. I was above average but still felt broke. Something was restless inside of me; something was missing. I did many of the right things to be successful—Maybe I didn't do all of them all of the time, but I did many of them.

I was sitting at one of those many motivational seminars I enjoy attending, listening to several multi-millionaires who are happy and successful, with balance in their lives. I wondered at that moment, "Why am I not up there as one of those successful people? I go to these workshops, I read, I do what most people don't or won't do, so what gives? Why am I in the audience and not up there?"

As I was thinking this, one of the speakers asked the audience a couple of questions. First he asked, "Do you think winning is possible?" I thought, "Well of course!" Then he asked, "If winning is possible, then why choose to lose?" That's when it hit me like a ton of bricks, like never before! I felt different that time, because finally the switch got flipped in the right direction! He was right: winning is a choice. Up to that point, I had chosen to be slightly above average versus going full tilt to pursue my dreams, and perhaps in the process helping others pursue theirs as well. I had been choosing to believe that I didn't deserve to be a huge success. Finally, it became crystal clear to me for the first time. I decided, "not anymore." I would no longer choose to be slightly above average! I chose to win, starting right then! I became consumed with feelings of gratitude and it felt extraordinary. I was thankful to the speaker, to the person who invited me to this seminar, to the people I met that day, and for being at the right place at the right time when I needed to hear that message. Then I started thinking about another idea. There were all those people that I was grateful to for helping me, so I need to return the favor. As Les Brown says, "You learn, you earn, and you pass it on!" This success thing isn't about just me; it's about others and being truly thankful for those who come into my life.

As I opened my heart even more than in the past and became unconditionally grateful for what is, the more the right people began to appear. I was able to start surrounding myself with the right people to help catapult me to the next level. I was also hopeful that I would be able touch their lives and do the same for them. This began to happen when I made the choice to win and to allow graciousness to perpetuate. I opened my door completely instead of half-way, and, the right people began to show up in my life. People will knock but you have to let them in!

I felt supercharged as never before. I had an internal energy that was amazing. This energy is infectious and attracts others into your life, others who also have it and others who need it to assist them in achieving their dreams. With every person I have met since that moment, there has been a mutual offering of ideas, thoughts, and assistance. These interactions are teaching me the power and producing results from having an enormous love for people and a great desire to serve. This has given me the results I have been looking for in my life: more equity in my business, peace of mind, better communication, unwillingness to settle for less than I desire, fearlessness in pursuing my dreams, and balance! I wake up happy and grateful everyday! It sounds wonderful doesn't it? It is, and I want to share it with others.

I can't tell you exactly when you might experience this deep gratitude. I know from my own experiences, however, the more you read, go to these seminars, and, most importantly, become grateful to those who come in and out of your lives, the sooner you will find your ideal life.

Michelle Quay

Your Gratitude Journal...The Gratitude Code!

Mario Turchetta

A few years ago, as an eager and struggling entrepreneur I learned something on the *Oprah Show* that would change my life forever. On the show she talked about writing down 5 things you were grateful for every night. Oprah called it the "Gratitude Journal." So from that day forth I started writing at least five things for which I was grateful for each day before going to bed. The first page started with ONE HUNDRED things, events or people I was grateful for in my life until then. One of those is Wayne Dyer who taught me how to meditate in a state of gratefulness every night. You start by writing in your gratitude journal and then meditate with those things in mind. Those two simple things together as a habit can dramatically improve your life and wellness. They can be **YOUR OWN GRATITUDE CODE!**

Find a nice book to write in, hard cover or leather bound, something of worth. Every night before we sleep Anne-Marie, my pearl and soul mate, starts at one end of the book, I start at the other end and we write our way towards the middle where we meet. The first thing I'm grateful for is Anne-Marie's LOVE. She is the reason I am where I am. Her love is the force that has the most impact on my life. Being with the right person makes life better and better every day. Then I write at least four more things for that day.

The Gratitude Code includes being grateful for those who touched you. Here are some examples:

I'm grateful for...

being coached by Best-Selling author Ray Vincent.

being part of a Mastermind Group.

being trained by Jack Canfield and Mark Victor Hansen.

my mom's help.

The Gratitude Code also includes being grateful for the people or person you've helped that day. I'm grateful for having the ability to help others. I've made it my mission in life. I'm using a principle that I've learned in business and in life:

Help other people get everything they want and you'll get everything you want! Have a "WHAT'S IN IT FOR THEM?" mentality.

Wake up... Live the Life You Love, Giving Gratitude

Here are some examples:

I'm grateful for...

helping Carole to reach her goal to stay at home with her kids.

helping Veronique with personal coaching.

helping children in third world countries go to school.

helping another family convert expenses into income while reducing or eliminating asthma, eczema and allergies.

Other times you may write things you are grateful for in more general terms such as:

I'm grateful for...

all the life-lessons I've learned.

my health.

the health of our friends and family.

playing soccer with kids today.

my friends and partners.

my little nephew Dario's smile.

To fully experience **The Gratitude Code,** create a Mastermind Group. Choose 8 to 10 people and get together once a week for breakfast. Start with a short morning meditation and ask each member to share for two minutes about good news or an accomplishment for the week. We use a **Victory Book** to record everyone's victories. After the good news we explore a best-selling book together, line by line. End with a gratitude meditation while concentrating on your blessings.

In your Gratitude Journal write something for each member every night. It can be accompanied by a wish that you want to help them materialize or manifest in their lives.

Here are some examples:

I Am Grateful For The Perfect Health And Peace Of Fernanda And Emidio By Divine Design.

I Am Grateful For The Perfect Health And The Ideal Man For Micheline By Divine Design.

I Am Grateful For The Perfect Health And The New Intergenerational House For Ray, Christine, Her Mom And The Kids By Divine Design.

Wake up... Live the Life You Love, Giving Gratitude

After you've written it out completely the first time, you can create a **Personal Gratitude Code** for each member by writing the first letter of each word while you repeat the sentences in your mind. Don't worry you can do this in less than 2 minutes when you memorize the code for each member. **IAGFTPHAPOFAEBDD. IAGFTPHATIMFMBDD.** Very soon you will know the code for each one by heart and *with heart*. Imagine having nine other people praying and manifesting for you.

When you go to bed at night thinking of all the blessings in your life, your brain is occupied with much nicer thoughts to nourish your dreams. You become what you think about. What if you could be dreaming about what you want all night long?

By focusing on the things for which you are grateful you will attract more things to be grateful for. Use the Gratitude Code. Start you Gratitude Journal tonight!

Thank heavens for the power of gratitude!

❧ Mario Turchetta

Why Am I Here?

Deepak Chopra
From an Interview with Dr. R. Winn Henderson

The majority of people on earth are unfulfilled or unhappy because they do not have a purpose or a mission. As a part of the human species, we seek purpose and meaning; we laugh, and we are aware of our mortality (that one day we will die). This is what distinguishes us from other creatures. Laughter, mortality and purpose become three important, crucial questions. We search for meaning—a deep significance to life.

Why am I here? Why have I been placed on the earth? We've been placed on earth to make a difference in life itself and in others' lives. In order to make a difference, we must find what we are good at, like to do, and benefits others.

We all have a mission, and my mission in life is to understand and explore consciousness and its various expressions and also to share that with anyone who's interested in doing the same. It boils down to understanding the mechanics of healing, the rule of love. I would say to put it very simply, my mission is to love, to heal, to serve and to begin the process of transforming both for myself and for those that I come in contact with.

As part of my mission, I founded The Chopra Center. My mission: to educate health professionals, patients and the general public on the connection between the relationship of mind, body, and spirit and healing. I teach people how to find their inner-self (most people have lost touch with theirs). When we find our inner-self, we find the wisdom that our bodies can be wonderful pharmacies—creating wonderful drugs. You name it, the human body can make it in the right dose, at the right time, for the right organ without side effects.

The body is a network of communication. Our thoughts influence everything that happens in our body. The problem is many people automatically assume, "All I have to do is think positively, and everything will be fine." Because many assume this, they become unnatural and pretend everything is okay.

Wake up... Live the Life You Love, Giving Gratitude

One must go beyond that; one must experience silence. It is when one experiences silence, healing energies become involved and a balance is created. Psalms 46:10 says, "Be still and know that I am God." When the body is silent, it knows how to repair itself.

Pursuing my mission gives me fulfillment. It makes me whole. It makes me feel that I will continue to do what I have been doing. If I had all the time and money in the world, this is what I would choose to do. It gives me joy and a connection to the creative bar of the universe. I have realized that the pursuit of my goals is the progressive expansion of happiness.

Pursue your goals and find your happiness, wholeness, and balance in this world.

cx Deepak Chopra, M.D.

My Biggest Gift!

Sharyn Abbott

I grew up stuttering until my sophomore year in high school. One day, my English teacher kept me after school, and made me read Shakespeare while holding my tongue. I was told years later that it was the most difficult way to stop stuttering, but since it worked for me, I never objected.

I discovered that when I made statements using a Southern drawl, such as "My daddy's from Texas," I somehow overcame my stuttering. This made me realize that I could change absolutely anything and everything just by working on it. From that point on, on each birthday, I chose a specific trait that I wanted to change or improve. I worked on improving my vocabulary, becoming a better conversationalist, accepting compliments, and not volunteering for everything, just to name a few. The list was very long!

I was very fortunate to marry a man who saw beyond my self-imposed limitations. He encouraged me to expand my horizons and when a national training position at a Fortune 500 company became available, he suggested that I take it. After two years of extensive travel, I had to choose whether to leave the company or to go into sales. I chose sales and managed to make the top ten every year.

After a severe back injury, I was told that I would have to have a steel rod placed in my spine and that I would need to be in a wheelchair for the rest of my life. While engaging in a desperate phone call with my father to discuss my lack of options, the phone book fell on the floor and opened to a page of ads for chiropractors. I called the largest ad on the page and made an appointment. Six months later, I was walking without any assistance.

In 1990, I cut my finger in a lawn mower and at the hospital the brand new emergency doctor gave me a tetanus shot with a specific antibiotic that caused Epstein-Barr virus. Over the next 12 years, this virus attacked every organ in my body.

My spleen failed first, and then my kidneys. I decided to try acupuncture. Thankfully, the treatment was successful and I totally

Wake up... Live the Life You Love, Giving Gratitude

recovered. Shortly after, I suffered a mild heart attack, and, in the third year of my illness, my pituitary gland became blocked, causing muscular dystrophy. I was not able to walk even a block for over five years. Then a friend introduced me to an American Indian shaman. He worked on me energetically every month for a year, and then every other month through the third year, at which time I was able to walk without difficulty. There were many other complications and just as many amazing alternative healers who kept me going when all others told me there was no hope.

One year later, I ended up with breast cancer. At this time, I felt that I had been dealt the last cryptic hand that I could possibly handle. That is when I was given yet one more miracle. I was given a Rife machine to use for two weeks. It is a machine that works on electrical energy, invented in 1935 by Dr. Royal Rife. Six weeks later, my cancer was completely gone.

I needed my work hours to be flexible so I started my own business helping entrepreneurs become better connected in their business community. It is exactly the business I would have designed if I had known it actually was a business. The training I had received from the Fortune firm was exactly what I needed to be successful in this venture. This business suits every aspect of my personality; the best part is that I get to help people solve their challenges every day.

Through my business associates, I have guided more than 200 people to alternative treatments that have lead to complete cures of ailments that they were told they would have to just live with.

I am who I am because of every experience that I've had. I am so grateful for each and every step, each and every lesson in my life. No matter what I experienced throughout the many traumas, the one thing that has come through loud and clear is that the biggest challenges in my life have been my biggest gifts.

∽ Sharyn Abbott

Wake up... Live the Life You Love, Giving Gratitude

It's Kind of Fun to Do the Impossible

Eileen Ashmore

Our spirit yearns for love, connection, meaning, excitement, and fulfillment. In our work lives, we want to have impact, to know that we have helped someone else and that we have made a difference. What is the secret to finding meaningful work such that we continue to grow and choose not to "retire" in our fifties or sixties? Some of the Boomer generation have retired at age 55. Are they really enjoying freedom at 55? How much travel, golf, art classes, gardening, reading, and volunteer work can we do before we need something that provides deeper meaning?

Over our 15, 20 and maybe even 30 years of work experience, we build a mosaic of skill, talent, and acumen that is hard to duplicate. As we think back on how our careers developed, we'll remember the 'aha' experiences that directed us to say, "Yes" to a new and challenging career direction. In my life, there have been five major career changes. These five careers have been in social work, teaching, professional sales, stock brokerage, and management consulting. Each time, I experienced excitement about the new career direction. And then, after a period of time, lack of promotion or financial reward or an unsupportive work environment increased my desire for improvement and fulfillment in my work life. For each career change, I was encouraged by someone in that career who was involved and passionate about their work.

Today, I feel grateful for the work I am doing. I am a management consultant working in the field of business and marketing strategy. Why do I get so excited about strategy and business planning? Why am I so fascinated with strategy and planning? It's hard to verbalize, but simply put, it's creating something with a client company that may never have existed before and which seems almost impossible to do. It takes courage, acumen, trust, and all of my past work experience, expertise, and education while working with a client team, to formulate a successful strategy. When a business or marketing strategy is well formulated and well executed, success is in the driver's seat. As the business becomes more successful, more excitement is created and the business is able to expand and hire more people. And then we strategize again! And again! And, it's fun! Walt Disney said it best when he said, "It's kind of fun to do the impossible." I agree!

I am deeply grateful for the honor and opportunity to work with my clients. They are intelligent, creative, dynamic, and caring people who make a difference. The execution of a well-formulated marketing strategy makes a world of difference to success. A well-formulated and focused business strategy sustains growth and profitability. Aligning the marketing strategy with the business strategy creates an unbeatable advantage. I'm glad and grateful to be part of each and every client team.

Once a colleague said to me, "More leads to more leads to more." I have learned that success's partner is prosperity. From prosperity flows income, work, and more opportunity for everyone. With the success of each individual business, success is created in our communities. The trickle-down effect of the success of each individual business provides prosperity and opportunity for all community members.

If you are wondering how to energize your career by finding the secret to meaningful work, here are two methods that will help you.

Method 1

Walk through a large bookstore and pick only the books (CD's, tapes, magazines, games, etc.) that you are drawn to. Take your time as you walk the aisles and carefully choose the books that draw your attention and interest. At the end of this exercise, you may have chosen 10 books or you may have chosen 100 books. Take some time to look at these books. Which ones command the most time? Which ones do you get lost in? These books reveal your natural interests and they show you where the seeds of your passion can be found.

Method 2

Set aside some time to think back over your life. Go right back to your first memories. What captured your attention? What thrilled you? Write it down. After you've done this, start piecing together all of these experiences. You'll begin to see your own mosaic of talent, skills, and acumen. You will begin to envision your next step toward what matters to you in your work life. It may be one of building on your current expertise, or, it may be something completely different from your past work experiences.

It involves risk to take your next step and you will encounter obstacles. To reduce your risks, take time to write down your plan, outline your goals and objectives and how you plan to execute the plan. Ask for divine guidance and then move forward.

If at first it feels as if you are challenged to do the impossible, take a leap of faith! Enjoy the process and may you experience the gratitude that provides energy, excitement, and fulfillment in your work and life. James Michener writes,

"If a man happens to find himself....he has a mansion which he can inhabit with dignity all the days of his life."

✧ Eileen Ashmore

In Gratitude

Melissa Boston

During my defining hour, I was paralyzed with procrastination. The passing of time became my enemy. I needed an assistant to take over my life. A drill sergeant who could make me put the pieces back together. I started to think about how people developed multiple personalities: since you can no longer depend on yourself to lead your own life you create the perfect person to come into your life and fix it. Most people cannot afford to hire a 24-hour assistant so some of them invent a version of themselves who is better, more organized and more efficient. Some might consider this "self improvement" and I see a very fine line between the two. My belief was, because I could still distinguish the difference, I was still on the side of sanity.

There you have it: The moment I woke up, in a nutshell. Waking up was fueled by the fear of never really waking up again. At the end of my life, I didn't want to look back to discover I had been sleep walking through most of it. We often walk a fine line between what's normal and what's not. Life was piling up on me fast and I had a choice to submit or to wake up.

As a kid, I watched my mom, Charlotte Lukes, who I love, respect and admire, work extremely hard. We were poor, but my brothers Vince (Dino) and Brian and sister Rebecca always had a roof over our heads and food to eat. One of the important concepts I grasped early on, which was passed down from my grandparents Melvin and Margaret Anderson, was to have a good work ethic. My grandfather worked a traditional job and my grandmother was a community advocator and leader in our town of Sparta, Illinois. My grandmother's influence is why I wanted to find a different way. I appreciated and respected her leadership and her ability to impact so many lives for the better.

Even when at the age of 19, I made the decision to become single mom; my family was in my corner. I still completed college in 4 ½ years, while working two jobs. Life after college afforded me a nice career, home, a nice car, a terrific son and what one would consider a nice life. I even purchased a home for my mother with cash.

But life didn't seem nice and the home and car didn't seem to matter so much when my spirit was suffering. God had planted in me something different. When your heart, mind and soul say one thing but you do another, you will eventually fail. I knew working for someone else was against everything God had planted inside of me. I wanted to own my life. Life changes in a series of moments. I knew I had to find that moment that would help me change the direction of my life.

When my defining moment came, I was almost too exhausted to allow it to make a difference. Life piled up on me quickly. But I found my inspiration through prayer, family and friends and by reading many books. I also fasted to purge out the 30 plus years of bad thoughts out of my mind, body and soul. Through it all, I emerged still breathing and became a better human being. My thoughts were clear and my spirit free. Through my belief there was a better way, I went on to impact the lives of thousands through business seminars and live conference calls. Through my belief I will go on to impact tens of thousands and possibly even millions of lives. If I can make a positive difference in the life of one, I have fulfilled my purpose.

There were moments I prayed for a drill sergeant when I had the two finest soldiers one could ask for on each side. I am grateful to my son, Tarique Rodgers for loving unconditionally. I judged, and Tarique loved and I thank God for blessing me with him. I am grateful to my fiancée Linus as well. He has always been there for me and I will spend my life being there for him. I am also grateful for the amazing friends I have met along the way: Nataya Williams, Dedrick Middleton, Katrina Greehill, Jerome Hughes and so many others have been instrumental to my success. I give thanks for my family: Lee Ann Rivera and Brian Walker, for seeing the vision when those around them did not.

I am thankful to be able to use my life in a way that serves others. I am grateful that I smile more than I frown and that I laugh more than I cry. I am grateful to God, grateful for family and friends and grateful for waking up.

℘ Melissa Boston

Right Place! Right Time
Marilyn Fitch

Gratitude ...Wow! When I look back on my life, I see how blessed I have been, even from my earliest days.

I have always been shy about being in front of a group. In high school I would never raise my hand to answer a question for fear I would say something wrong and be humiliated. Because of my shyness, I was worried that I would never be able to go to a job interview. Luckily I didn't have to: my principal called me into his office just before graduation and said, "A medical/dental office is looking for a receptionist and I have recommended you." I did not even have to go for an interview and I started work the week after graduation.

A few years later, while bowling with my girlfriend, I met my wonderful future husband. Nine months after meeting we were married and two years later we became the proud parents of a son. My husband is responsible for building my self-confidence for the past 43 years. If ever I say, "I don't think I can do this" his response is always, "Honey, I know you can!" I am so thankful that I was at the bowling alley, in the "Right Place at the Right Time," to meet my lifetime partner and soul mate.

When my husband graduated from college, we moved to San Diego and I had the privilege of being a stay-at-home mom. I started a part-time home-based typing service and, over the next 17 years, I typed many masters and doctoral theses. One day, as I was picking up supplies for my typing service, the owner of the dealership asked if I knew anyone who was looking for an accounting position. I had just taken a refresher course in bookkeeping, which had been my favorite subject in high school, so my reply was, "How about me?" I was hired and remained with that company for the next 20 years, until I retired. Again all this happened in the "Right Place at the Right Time."

When we first moved to San Diego, I became very active in Beta Sigma Phi, a cultural and philanthropic international sorority. This was a confidence-building experience for me. My sorority sisters admitted that when I first visited their chapter, they were not sure whether I would fit in because I was so quiet. However, they were fully supportive of me and I was elected president of our chapter several times. I also served as president of the sorority area council, Tierra del Sol Area Council of Beta Sigma Phi. This experience was a tremendous help in teaching me leadership skills.

I believe that throughout all those years, whenever I needed a change in my life, I was always in the "Right Place at the Right Time."

Only two weeks into my retirement, my friend, Carol Young, volunteered us to help with a vendor table for "It's All About the Kids" at the first Wake-Up Summit to be held in San Diego. After listening to the first two dynamic speakers, we decided to stay for the "Wake-Up" luncheon. The meal was served buffet style and most of the seats were already filled. We happened to sit right next to Ann Preston, CEO of Freedom Builders, Inc. We became very interested in what she had to offer and scheduled an appointment with her following the afternoon sessions. All my life I had wanted to help business people and friends become more successful. I knew right away that this new "career" would be a lot more fun than being retired. I have always had a passion for networking and have been involved, on a part-time basis, with several different networking companies. Now I can connect businesses through "netstorming," a technique that can help businesses become more successful. We have what we call a "Unique Business System," which I love sharing with others.

In Freedom Builders, we teach ways to build trusting relationships within the business environment. This is one of the components of our Unique Business System. We know that people want to give and receive trustworthy referrals.

For all my achievements, I am truly grateful and I thank the Good Lord for having me in the "Right Place at the Right Time." When a person is giving and willing to help others, goodness will eventually come back to them in some way. A person should give thanks, but never give up—even if they are as shy and bashful as I was.

ᴄⱷ Marilyn Fitch

Giving With a Passion
John Hall

*T*he most profound discovery I've made about my life in this world is this: it's not about me.

Life is not centered on my goals, my ambitions, my peace of mind, my plans, my money, or my toys. I wasn't created to serve myself, and I will never find who I am or what my destiny is to be by looking in the mirror.

Real living is about giving to others; giving for the sake of giving, without regard for what may come in return; making the choice to give as a lifestyle—with a passion.

This perspective makes all the difference. Our search for meaning, our search for significance, our search for purpose finds focus when we choose to give to others.

Real giving isn't just about money. It's about giving ourselves— our knowledge, our wisdom, our talents, our time—investing in the lives of others. This lifestyle does not need to revolve around a legalistic system of plans and percentage calculations. Rather, it revolves around simply looking at the needs of those with whom we come in contact and reaching out with what we have been given.

Giving is not necessarily an expensive thing to do, either. We are all wealthy in different ways, so giving can be as inexpensive as a smile, a sincere "thank you," a word of encouragement or saying "how are you?" to a total stranger—and meaning it.

Each encounter throughout every day of our lives presents an opportunity to contribute something beneficial to the life of another person. Every encounter is unique and none are coincidental. Just as there are no unimportant people, there are also no unimportant encounters. Thus, there is no unimportant giving.

From this kind of giving comes a sense of mission in life: A sense of motivation that, for each of us, there is indeed a higher calling. And from this comes a basis for answers when we ask ourselves the big life questions, like who we are to be and what we are to do. From this we derive a level of satisfaction that is unequalled by self-serving pursuits.

We soon learn that giving of ourselves in small ways prepares us for the privilege and the responsibility of giving in bigger ways—in ways that change the lives of other people. This is what will ultimately define who we are and what our legacy will be.

We find ourselves by giving to others—with a passion.

છ John Hall

Gratitude
Ida Greene, RN, LMFT, Ph.D.

*L*ooking back at my childhood, growing up as a black person in Pensacola, Florida, I was hard-pressed to find anything for which I was grateful. We were very poor. I never had lunch money for school, and I had to walk ten miles to and from school. I grew up in a segregated city where I had to ride on the back of the bus, drink from a "colored-only" public water fountain, and attend a segregated school with inferior books and educational supplies. We could not eat at the lunch counter in the downtown department store. When my mother took us to buy shoes, I could not put my foot inside the shoe for fitting; instead I had to place my foot outside the shoe and let the salesman guess my shoe size. My mother always bought our shoes a half size larger so that we could wear them longer.

When I was 14, I was sexually molested by a white man when I would clean house for his wife. After I told my father what happened, he did not let me go back. We could not report things like that to the police, for the report would have been thrown in the trash. Also, my father could have been beaten by the police for making a false claim if the man denied touching me. I watched in pain and anger as my dad would scratch his head and say, "yes sir, and no sir," to all white men regardless of their age. I was very angry with white men for humiliating my dad and, in doing so, taking away his dignity. I vowed never to let any white person take away my self-esteem and self-respect. I was also angry that no white person in Pensacola had the courage to speak up against the unjust Jim-Crow practices of injustice against blacks.

My mother had a third-grade education, and she could not read or write. She would have to mark an "X" on anything that required her signature. I taught her how to write her name. My mother had a thirst for education but because she had to work in the fields to help her family buy food, she could not go to school. Her desire to have an education became a passion that she instilled in me. Everyday of my life I heard, "Get an education; that is something no one can take away from you." As I watched all of the injustices against black people, my anger and defiance swelled. I knew that I could possibly be killed because I would always move from the back to the front of the bus. I was determined that I would leave Pensacola as soon as I graduated from high school.

These experiences taught me how to take charge of my destiny; to resolve that no one else would decide who or what I could become. I learned how to turn my lemons into lemonade and to see roadblocks as temporary inconveniences. I am not actually grateful for those painful experiences. They helped me to develop the fortitude and strength of character that I needed when I applied to attend the all —white Grady Nursing School in Georgia and was told that I failed the entrance test. I then decided to go to Chicago and to apply to attend Provident School of Nursing, the facility at which Dr. Daniel Hale Williams was the first physician, black or white, to perform open heart surgery.

I was accepted into the all black school of nursing. After I attended school for one year, I ran out of money. I am very grateful to the State of Illinois for paying my tuition and giving me a small stipend during my junior and senior year so I could remain in school.

My decision to become a Registered Nurse was the best decision I ever made. I continued my education, obtained a bachelor's degree in psychology and a master's degree in counseling. I am a licensed marriage and family therapist and I have a teaching credential and a Ph.D. in theology. In addition, I am now certified as a hypnotherapist, and a Reiki practitioner and a life coach. I am very proud of all that I have been able to accomplish. My background is now actually something for which I can be grateful. I am grateful for the fact that I can learn, grow, and develop my inner potential.

೧౨ Ida Greene

Wake up... Live the Life You Love, Giving Gratitude

A Wonderful Life with My Soul Mate

C. John Yeo

I must start this true story as I recall it from the morning of the day I met Ollie at 10:05 p.m. on July 7, 1991, at St. Vladimir's dance hall. We danced for 12 years, 9 hours and 20 minutes.

When my day started, I did not want to go to work, but I did anyway. That evening, it would be my usual Friday night of music lessons, playing piano and singing. Then I would go late to the singles dance, usually arriving just before the mixers dance at the halfway break.

After work I thought, "What's the use of going to the dance late?" Then, on the way to my lessons, I was still not very happy. But after singing a few songs I suddenly felt much happier and thought, "I might as well go to the dance; it's not very far."

I arrived just as the band leader announced the mixer dance and asked the men to line up on one side of the room and the ladies on the other. I joined the end of the line, the music started and the lines began to move together. The first partner I danced with I cannot recall.

The next one was a lovely lady in a flowing yellow dress. She had a very happy, smiling face, and the first thought that entered my mind was "I could spend the rest of my life with this woman." The clock on the wall behind her read 10:05 p.m.

Her name was Ollie, and as we started our first steps she asked, "How many children do you have?" I answered, "My late wife wanted six boys and I wanted a girl, but we never had any."

Ollie just laughed very happily. She said, "I have six boys and one girl!" Putting some wonderful energy into the dance, we held each other. We continued dancing until the end of the music, when, by custom, we should have separated to take new partners. For whatever reason, we were not parted and we were together from that time on.

That night we made our first date to meet for a sandwich lunch in her office. As time passed we spent most of the evenings together at Ollie's home. After a few weeks, Ollie arranged a dinner with all of her sons and her daughter. I was so blessed that day to go from being alone to joining a family of eight.

Times seemed to float by and Ollie and I married on June 26th, 1993. The years were better and more enjoyable than ever, until the day we played Ollie's last golf game. The sign for Ollie was the tee shot on the third tee. Two friends and I watched as Ollie gave her usual smooth swing sending the ball straight and true. As we watched her complete the back swing we all heard a "crack" and saw Ollie holding her left arm. She had dislocated her left shoulder. That was Ollie's last golf swing.

X-rays showed her shoulder was partly out of its socket, but the x-ray included her lungs and doctors found other signs there. More tests confirmed the doctors concerns that cancer was present.

We spent the next four weeks going for other tests until, finally, we went to the cancer clinic for the final evaluation on the July 10, 2003. They gave Ollie a room and I stayed with her. Each night I slept on a cot on the floor beside the bed until she was sent to the hospice centre.

I spent some of the days and all of the nights with Ollie. Her family and friends visited during the daytime. On the final Sunday Ollie enjoyed all of her family. When I arrived in the afternoon, Ollie looked at me, raised her right hand and blew me a kiss; I blew one in return. One of the daughters-in-law said, "What a lovely gesture! That's the most activity we have seen all afternoon."

That night she went into a deep sleep. In the early morning, at 7:10, I called the nurse. I had the privilege of seeing Ollie for the last few seconds of her journey on earth. I stooped down and looked into her eyes and said, "You are going on a beautiful spiritual journey and all of your family loves you. I love you very much and God loves you. I must say good bye."

At the exact time I said, "Good-bye," her pupils dropped from my gaze to the corners of her eyes. I stood, cradled her head, and said, "Ollie has gone." The time was 7:25 a.m.

There are many things in the universe that we may never fully understand but if we live our lives with love in our hearts, miracles can happen. You can create a miracle for yourself, if you will do as Ollie used to say to her clients:

"Love yourself a little more each day. Before going to bed each day, look in the mirror and focus on your pupils and say, 'I love you, I love you, I love you.' Do this for 21 days, and you will notice a pleasant change in yourself."

I am so grateful for having Ollie in my life. So, thank you for reading my story. Because of you, I have had the chance to live it all again. Even in memory, it is still wonderful.

With light and love to you,

ↄ C. John Yeo

Wake up... Live the Life You Love, Giving Gratitude

Getting More through Gratitude
Jase Souder

Do you want more in your life? Do you want to enjoy life more? Do you want abundance? If you said, "Yes," to one or more of the questions above then we should look, together, at being grateful.

"Grateful?" you ask? Yes, grateful. Being grateful is what opens up the door for more.

Take a moment and think about the things you want in your life. Take just a minute and think of everything you want. Do it now: make a list.

If you did the work you probably have quite a list of things you want and don't have. But, did you list the things you already have? To become more abundant you must appreciate and be grateful for how much abundance you already have. If you don't want what you already have you may not hold on to it, and you certainly won't open up space for more.

Wanting and being grateful for what we've got is the key to opening up our lives for more.

Step 1. Be grateful for what we have!

My seminar company is growing and I'm turning over the running of the seminars to my team of coaches, speakers and employees. At a recent seminar being led by another coach we had some breakdowns in the running of the seminar; some of the things were not done the way I would want and expect. While I didn't appreciate having breakdowns, within 24 hours I found myself in a place of gratitude: I would much rather have these breakdowns now, while the company is small and I'm at the seminar, than years from now when the company is huge and I'm not available.

To put it another way, when I go to take on a new challenge there is a part of me that secretly hopes I'll fail. I know that if I fail at something I'll redouble my efforts and my learning and then make the attempt a second time. I know that if I fail, learn more and then try again, I'll perform better than if I had simply succeeded the first time.

Failures cause us to learn and improve.

Step 2. Be grateful for setbacks.

Finally, in all of life, including sales, gratitude helps us get more.

I used to be involved in Big Brothers/Big Sisters. One day I gave my little brother a one dollar bill. He gave me back a half hearted "thanks." Immediately I started to regret giving him the bill, feeling like he wasn't appreciative. So I said to him, "When people give you money, be grateful; say, 'Thank you, thank you, thank you,' so that they are happy they gave you money." Then I gave him another dollar bill. His eyes lit up, he held the dollars up in his hands and sang, "Thank you, thank you, thank you," while bouncing in his seat. He was so cute I pulled out a five dollar bill and gave it to him. He started bouncing around his seat like popcorn in an air popper.

The point of my story is that in negotiations, sales or relationships, if you are not grateful, people will stop giving. If you choose to be grateful when people give you what you want, they'll tend to give you more of what you want.

Step 3. Be grateful for what you get and you'll get more.

                                       ભ Jase Souder

Being Grateful for Now

Steven E.

We seem to get caught up living in either the past or the future. We need to focus on the present moment. When we keep our power in the present, we become more attuned to our life and to our surroundings.

The next time you are washing the dishes, watch the water come out of the faucet and the bubbles rise in the water. Pay attention to your hands washing the dishes. Absorb yourself in the moment and not on how to maneuver tomorrow.

Start being aware of your thoughts. Your intentions create the reality you are living. Until you become aware of this, it happens unconsciously. Now, close your eyes and picture the current life situation, your relationships, finances, job and family.

Open your eyes. Find yourself in the moment and know that you have created your whole life consciously or unconsciously. Live your life in the present and **create the life that you love**. It is so easy to be grateful for the simple beauty; the common miracle of your life right now.

At birth, your subconscious mind begins to record your every feeling, thought and word, and you accepted whatever your parents and teachers told you. Those who taught you their beliefs probably loved you dearly and did the very best they could. You learned their ways, their weaknesses and limitations, their fears, self-guilt and sins along with the positive messages they tried to relay to you.

I realized that 95 percent of what I learned as a child were the limitations of other people. And we hold on to many of these beliefs about self-worth, our body, our attractiveness, our goodness and our finances. All these beliefs came from somewhere. NOW, they are our reality; they are the truth about you, and you hold onto them very tightly.

What we believe creates our world and our reality. Now is the time to leave behind all your old self-defeating and destructive beliefs. Get rid of them! Listen to your own heart. Learn to forgive yourself and realize that we punish ourselves for our so-called sins.

Wake up... Live the Life You Love, Giving Gratitude

Realize that sin is self-inflicted nonsense. Forgive yourself; thank yourself; love yourself.

We become what we think and feel about ourselves. If we think from fear and limitation, we imprison ourselves. When we learn to sit quietly and go within, we find our true self and discover peace; we find our true and free and loving spirit.

This process will rid us of our old negative beliefs. This freedom will take us beyond mass thinking, which is programmed by fear and limitations. When we listen to our inner selves we will live a life that we love, and we will live it in the now.

ल Steven E

My First Home Birth
Teri Schulte

*M*y husband, Tony, and I were planning our first home birth after having our daughter, April, in a hospital, just seventeen months earlier. At that time, rooming-in with your baby was allowed only from 9:00 A.M. to 9:00 P.M., and April was born in the middle of the night. After I had had only twenty minutes with her, the nurses came and took her to the nursery to weigh and measure her. That was more important to them than allowing babies to bond with their parents. They said that I needed my rest, but sleep was the last thing on my mind. I had waited nine months to have my baby in my arms and get to know her. Regardless of my pleas, they would not bend their rules. I waited six long hours for them to bring my baby back so that I could finish feeding her, count her toes, and just enjoy holding her. With my next pregnancy I was determined to have my baby at home. I was very grateful that my husband quickly agreed.

At 4:00 A.M., I awoke and I knew with an urgent certainty that my second child was on the way. Now that we were having our first home birth, our midwife was out of town at a seminar! She had said the baby would most likely wait until she returned, but that just wasn't happening. Tony called the midwives' service to have them find another midwife for us. He then started getting the room ready and called family members to tell them that the birth would be soon.

My contractions were seven minutes apart. The pain was intense. Then I remembered, from our Bradley childbirth class, that I needed to accept what was happening to my body and work with it. I knew that the end result from all this discomfort would be a precious baby in my arms. I had to adjust my attitude and begin the abdominal breathing that we had learned. I started thinking, "OK...I can do this."

We were glad that labor was progressing quickly, but were a little nervous because we still didn't have a midwife to attend the birth. By this time my parents and sister had arrived, but none of us knew how to "catch a baby!"

After only two hours of labor and contractions that were two minutes apart, my midwife's assistant arrived. She examined me and told me that I was in transition (the hardest part of labor) and that I was almost fully dilated. We were so very grateful when the midwife, Donna, arrived. She was very helpful and knew exactly what to do. It was as if she came in and swept the room free of all worries, doubts, and fears!

When my mom and my sister heard me say, "He's coming," they rushed into the bedroom to watch the birth. I turned on my side while holding onto Tony's arm very tightly and pushed our baby out with two strong contractions. Someone said, "It's a boy!" Donna suctioned his nose and throat, and then laid him on my belly. What a wonderful way to have a baby! Timothy Paul was born three hours and twenty minutes after labor began.

About twenty minutes after his birth, we took Timmy to the kitchen sink and gave him a LeBoyer bath, which he very much enjoyed. He was so happy and alert as he kicked and splashed in the water. I had a quick shower and then April woke up and joined us on the bed to see her new little brother. She could not kiss him enough. She was so excited!

What a blessing it was to have Timmy at home, with loved ones all around to welcome him into the family. How grateful we were to be able to make our own choices regarding his birth, especially for the fact that we could immediately begin family bonding. We thanked the Lord for a short labor, a gentle birth, a great attending midwife, and a beautiful and healthy baby boy. All of our prayers had been answered. It was an exciting and memorable way to bring a baby into the world.

ఴ Teri Schulte

An Attitude of Gratitude – the Thing
I Am Most Grateful for in My Life

K. Carl Smith

I can clearly recall a father-and-son conversation I had with my Dad after losing a football game. At the time I was in the sixth grade and was the starting quarterback for my middle school team. We were carrying a perfect 6-zero record into the final game of the regular season, expecting to go undefeated into the playoffs. Apparently, we were bursting with over-confidence because we played terribly. I don't remember us ever crossing the 50-yard line. Afterwards, to put it plainly, I was angry. I was upset about the loss and embarrassed by my lackluster performance. I felt my life had come to a sudden stop. I made up my mind not to play in the post-season.

Later that evening my father sat me down and put me in check (I love those "teachable moments" with Dad). He said, "Son, I know you are sad about losing the game but it seems to me there are some questions you need to ask yourself about the game of life. Do you know what you want? What price are you willing to pay to make your dreams come true? Do you know what your strengths are? Are you a person who quits when things don't go your way? Are you giving 100% of your God-given talents while trying to overcome disappointments and limitations? A part of being a winner involves learning how to rebound from defeat. Learn from your failures, put them behind you, and press on." Well, I did press on. In fact, I played in the remaining games and led my team to a championship season.

I am overwhelmingly grateful for that childhood experience because it served as a launch pad for my life. It taught me a valuable lesson regarding the power of purpose and passion and forced me to examine my attitude.

Purpose. I learned that having a purpose in life is all about God allowing us to do something for Him. The absence of a personal mission leads to fear, doubt, havoc, misery, and self pity, all of which lead to failure. Success does not come about by accident, but it begins with discovering the reason we are here. People without a sense of purpose are like a fly at a family reunion picnic; they see lots of opportunity but can't decide where to start. Discovering your purpose is the key for living a rewarding life.

Passion. I define passion as an inner force that pulls us to succeed. It is the "power source" for all achievement. When we are passionately doing what we love, success is in the making because passion won't allow us to surrender. It gives us the drive and inspiration to achieve the gifts of our heart against all odds. "There is one quality which one must possess to win," said Napoleon Hill, "and that is a definiteness of purpose, the knowledge of what one wants, and a burning desire to possess it."

Attitude. Successful people know challenging events, misfortune, and adverse situations are inevitable. How we respond to the circumstances is a matter of choice—our attitude. Simply put, when our attitude is correct, our perception is positive, our abilities reach maximum effectiveness, and we transform adversity into an opportunity. Life situations may shape our outlook, but we have the God-given power to choose the outcome. Purpose-driven people know that attitude is a prerequisite for success and they make the most of the situation.

- They do more than they are paid to do.
- They give a little more than expected.
- They try a little harder.
- They aim a little higher than they think is possible.

A positive attitude can change what tomorrow brings!

The Creator has given us much for which to be grateful. He has placed in each of us a genius waiting to live out its purpose. First, we must decide what we like to do. Second, we must make passion our companion through life's journey. Finally, we must remain continually optimistic in the face of difficulty. The choice is yours. THINK of what life has to offer you. DO what makes you happy. BE the best you can be. Enjoy the journey!

ↄ K. Carl Smith

She Believed in Me

Anthony Treas

The person I am most grateful for is my high school teacher, Ms. Virginia Panttaja.

I went into high school with no self-esteem whatsoever. This may be true for a lot of freshman, but, if there was a meter for self-esteem, I would not have even registered on the scale.

Ms. Panttaja was my personal development teacher my freshman year. This was a class that was being offered for the first time, and most people who took it were looking for an easy "A." I'm not sure why I chose it from all the courses I could have taken.

On the first day of class, Ms. Panttaja took me under her wing. She could see how unmotivated I was. She began to encourage me and, in doing so, helped me to develop a belief in myself. She knew that my father was an alcoholic and she realized how important it was for me to let go of my hurt. She shared with me a quote from Eleanor Roosevelt: "No one can hurt you without your consent."

I began to believe that I could accomplish anything I set my mind to and my positive attitude continued to grow throughout my high school career. I joined the NJROTC and at the end of my junior year was asked by Captain John "Nick" Nicholson, my commanding officer, to be the Commander of the unit my senior year. This is the highest rank a student can receive. I would not have been able to accomplish this without the belief I had in myself, and I give all the credit to Ms. Panttaja. She was so proud of me when I was selected to be the next Commander.

Because of Ms. Panttaja I was able to radically change the course of my life. Even now, when I am going through hard times, I look back and recall how much Ms. Panttaja believed in me and how proud she was of me. Now, it is my turn to teach others to believe in themselves and to show them that they can change the course of their lives. I am an example of that and so is my father, who is now a recovering alcoholic. Today, my father and I have the best relationship a son and father could have. Again, I give credit to Ms. Panttaja and the principles I learned from her.

For your free gift, go to: **www.wakeupand.com**

What Ms. Panttaja did for me, she did for the hundreds of other young people. I hope that she realizes what an impact she has made in the world. I am so grateful to have had such an incredible teacher. The principles she taught me and the positive attitude she helped me cultivate have helped me accomplish a life's dream: to be an author. I still have the graduation card she gave me. On the card, as always, she expressed her belief in me. As a postscript she wrote, "Remember you can do and be anything you want."

I am now a personal life coach, a mentor, a motivational speaker, and a writer. I get the chance to inspire people to overcome what they perceive to be obstacles to the accomplishment of their goals. Now I understand why I took that class. It was my mission in life.

ഇ Anthony Treas

The Three Realms of Success
Luther Blalock

Should we truly wake up and live a life we love? Does that sound like a silly question? Then why do most of us go through life living a suboptimal existence?

We do so, primarily, because we haven't examined our lives to learn how to energize our most basic, core values. This process takes time. After years of searching, true success for me has come down to three areas of living. These are the spiritual, mental, and physical life. So how does one succeed in all three areas? I humbly submit that it is by practicing daily the principles of total acceptance and applied wisdom that we find the binary code of abundant living.

I am thankful I learned that I must totally accept the universe and life as they are; the good and the bad. There will always be great opportunities and there will always be imperfection and injustice. Until we stop trying to change the rules of life, we will not succeed. Rules? Yes, such as, "You reap what you sow," and, "Do unto others as you would have them do unto you." Looking—really looking—for opportunities to apply these two simple rules with others everyday, will change your life. We are grateful when someone helps us, but we should be equally thankful for the opportunity to serve others.

Applying wisdom in daily living for me has come to mean learning from mistakes and not repeating them. It also means being wise enough to feed my soul, mind, and body "premium nutrition." Good books, good people, and good food are premium nutrition. There are two aspects to wisdom: learning and taking action. Learning great lessons and insights are useless if they don't change one's behavior. Will we be perfect at this? No. Some lessons are learned a number of times before they sink in and change actions.

Hey, what about financial success? Isn't that what most people think about when they think of a person as a success? Well, until you are successful in the three realms of life, you are not ready for financial success. "For what does it profit a man to gain the whole world and lose his own soul?" I learned this the hard way. If you are not grounded in solid values, if you don't have what Robert Allen calls a big enough "Why," you'll find yourself floundering in your efforts or perhaps fulfilling that famous saying, "Easy come, easy go."

I would like to make a personal recommendation for a book I found to be an outstanding guide. I came full circle back to this book over a period of time. This book contains the core elements of every good idea you'll ever encounter: The Bible.

Finally, I have some thoughts to share on each of these areas of life.

Spiritually speaking, the ultimate guide to success is "Love God with all your heart, and all your mind, and all your strength. And love your neighbor as yourself." A life based on this premise cannot fail.

Mentally, the key is to always monitor your attitude and to truly believe that you can get to where you want to be. The great Earl Nightingale said, "We become what we think about."

Physically, we could modify a previous saying, "What good is it to gain the whole world and lose your physical health?" You have to make a decision to adjust your exercise and diet to attain premium living with the energy so vital to a successful life.

I would love to hear from like-minded individuals. I would be grateful for the chance: Let's share some life!

ᴇↄ Luther Blalock

How Will You Be Remembered?

Victoria Baker

"And be not conformed to this world;
but be ye transformed by the renewing of your mind…"
Romans 12:2 (KJV)

A desire to renew my spirit led me to visit the cemetery where my mother, grandparents, and other relatives are buried. A wave of gratitude filled my heart for the nurturing environment they provided. Their purpose was to create a better life for generations to follow. How will you be remembered after your passing? Examine your life by asking, "Am I living a life with purpose?"

You have the power to alter events by transforming negative energy into a positive event: a memory. As I sat in the cemetery, loving memories filled my heart taking me back to happier times in my childhood. I reminisced of the family gatherings that brought us closer. In those days children were meant to be seen and not heard. Nonetheless, you got a good sense of right and wrong. Through observation, you learned a level of respect. I always thought of my family as leaders and role models, along with the teachers, police, firemen, and clergy. I did not need a comic book super hero since I had living breathing examples of how to live my life.

Make a difference in your life by making a difference in the life of a child, or someone less fortunate than yourself. As a child I was taught to perform good deeds without expecting rewards. If you offered someone payment, usually no one accepted it. You were expected to come to someone's aid if given the opportunity to help.

The neighborhood where I lived took care of the children by providing a safe haven. We learned community service as an integral part of our upbringing, that is; to be of service to others, have respect for others as well as ourselves, and to be humble and not boastful. These were expectations given to improve our family and our community by developing us as leaders. Where will tomorrow leaders come from if not from our youth?

Gratitude is an individual, unselfish devotion of your time to pursue a path with a purpose. It was understood that to live a rich life meant more than just accumulating wealth. Owning a house was more important than having a vehicle; a house was to build a home where every individual in the family could have access to important amenities. It was a place where each child was prepared to go out into the world to face the challenges of life. It took such an environment to mold children into individuals who would make a difference in the lives of others, for none of us prospered if any of us were in need.

As children, we were taught a set of values which, even when we thought they were forgotten, would resurface at the appropriate time as a reflection of our learning. We learned that "please" and "thank you," "Yes, Madam," and "No, Sir" were to be part of our vocabulary. We were taught that there were protocols and etiquette that were unquestionably part of our being. We understood that we were on Earth for a purpose and must seek that purpose with that burning desire unique to us all.

We were constantly asked what we wanted to be when older. This gave us direction and a sense of the future. We were encouraged to see beyond ourselves and be prepared for the harsh and bitter times that come with life. Hence, we knew that part of living required the courage to persevere, and to endure hardships. It was important as a model of leadership. The needs of others are so great—some so seemingly insurmountable—yet, there are people who dedicate their lives to providing an opportunity for others to not merely survive, but to enhance their lives to the fullest. Helping those who had less was beneficial to all. It came to the simple question: "How do you make your life count for something?"

What are we teaching our children? I come into contact with children and youth who have no direction, no goals for the future. Some do not even feel they will make it out of high school. No one has taken the time to really listen; to communicate to them that there is a way to make their dreams come true without criminal behavior. There is a wholeness that is missing and it only takes a moment for a child to make a decision that affects the rest of his life. What legacy do we leave our children?

Wake up... Live the Life You Love, Giving Gratitude

What am I grateful for? Most of us do not contemplate this question until Thanksgiving dinner. For others it may be part of daily meditation or prayer. Each day that I open my eyes I am grateful for just another day. It is another opportunity to transform each day in a way that is positive and full of purpose. I am grateful for those individuals who nurtured me as a child, preparing me for the future. I choose each day to make a difference not only in my life, but also in the lives of others. So, ask yourself, "How will I be remembered?" Take the time to gratefully transform your life into the one you want.

ల Victoria L. Baker

Gratitude and the Old Buick

Tim McMurray

Gratitude, by its very nature, implies a feeling that should happen "after" something else.

For example: you need help, you get help, and therefore you feel grateful for those who helped. But, have you ever been grateful for something that hasn't happened yet? Have you ever *projected* gratitude into the future?

Webster tactfully defines gratitude as a "state of appreciation and gratefulness; i.e., thankfulness." However, my introduction to gratitude came not from a dictionary, but from a life lesson I will never forget.

Several years ago I found myself broken—at the end of a series of bad breaks, deals and decisions. The problem was, this was my *third* time to find myself in this position. Third time's the charm: This time I had gone out with a bang, losing a company valued at $15 million.

Any married man or father will understand when I say that it's painful to look in the eyes of your wife and children when you feel you have failed them. I try to do everything spectacularly, and even my failures fit my criteria: I was foreclosed upon, my vehicles were repossessed; nothing was sacred to the bank. Children look to their father for leadership, and my five children, ranging in age from five to 15, did in fact look to me for answers and direction with questions that grown men and women ask themselves every day: Why me? Why us?

With help from church members and friends, we managed to move to a home one-third the size of our prior homes. A friend, knowing our plight, told me of an old car which had been owned by his recently deceased uncle: a 1976 Buick Le Sabre two door coupe.

The Old Buick had been parked for five years under a tree in East Texas; had the rusty imprint of a child's hand on the hood, etched into the metal; and the shocks were so bad that the car squeaked continuously on the road. When stopped, it would continue to bounce wildly, loudly coming to rest after an excruciating couple of minutes.

The children were mortified. Even worse, the car was as cranky as a scorned woman: sometimes it would start, and sometimes it wouldn't.

On those occasions, the kids would add insult to injury, demanding to know *why* they had to endure both the "piece of junk" car and its erratic behavior.

I had to keep a good face on things, so I'd say, "Kids, we must speak kindly of the Old Buick. We have to be grateful that we have something that will take us where we're going." At that point, I'd pat the dashboard and say, aloud, "Good Buick! I am so thankful that you are running so *well!*"

My kids will testify to this: *Nine out of 10 times, the car would start instantly, and run the rest of the time!*

I came to trust in the Old Buick like one would a grizzled but dependable sea captain in dangerous waters. Then came the day when, while riding with a business partner, the old Buick simply died; no power, no cranking, not even a smoking back-fire. Of course, I tried my same routine: *"Good Buick, I am so thankful that you are running so well!"* Pat. Pat. Pat.

Viola! The engine roared—and so did I! Was it a miracle? I prefer to think that it was the power of *grateful appreciation* at work.

When we appreciate something, or someone, that person or thing inherits a much greater value in our minds. Taken quite literally: To appreciate something is to be aware of it, and to *increase* its price or value. Real estate, for example, *appreciates* because it is *appreciated.* Demand and value increase in equal proportion.

Are not our families and friends among the *assets* of our lives? Even strangers can be appreciated if we pay attention to them, and what they say. Clark Kent and Superman were, after all, the same guy; the only difference is in how they were *packaged* and *perceived.*

I kept the Old Buick for 3 years. As my fortunes improved, I installed new bushings to stop the squeaking. I bought new shocks, redid the interior, rebuilt the motor, provided fresh paint and the 10-disc CD player. Slowly, the car began to transform. Imagine her absolute glee when I tacked on a Class III trailer hitch and bought a 25-foot Master Craft ski boat for her to tow!

No longer did the kids duck in the backseat. We drove proudly to the lake in our $800 Buick, with our $40,000 boat in tow. Our family would exchange knowing glances when people ask, "*Why are you pulling that awesome boat with that old junk car?*"

"Because," I would answer, eyes twinkling, "*I have my priorities right!*"

In that life experience, our children learned a valuable lesson about gratitude. One day in church, my oldest son shared the story of the old Buick and how it had made him *appreciate* even those things we don't initially trust or value. "The old Buick," he said, "and those experiences … were worth far more than if our family had owned a Rolls Royce the entire time."

I challenge you to think of someone who is close to you, albeit a spouse, child, mother, father, brother or sister, even a friend. Think of 30 things you appreciate about them. Place one thing per day on a calendar, and I'll bet you will be startled by how *fast* they appreciate.

The story of the old Buick, in the end, is a story of irony and discovery. It's the story of how I started from one place, and ended up at quite another, learning and teaching as I went. That Old Buick transported me to places I could never have imagined as I gazed at it, abandoned under that lone tree in East Texas, so many years ago.

I have created what I call an "Appreciation Calendar" for the love of my life, the mother of my children and my eternal partner. My heart fills with sincere gratitude every day for the gift of herself that she has given me in the last thirty five years. Above everything in my life, I value and appreciate the one who sat beside me in that Old Buick, every mile of the way: Susan McMurray, my bride, and my soul-mate.

ల Tim McMurray

Being Grateful For It All

Elizabeth Menzel

Disclaimer:

I realize that writing about Oneness/Unity Consciousness/God/All That Is/The Beloved is impossible. The very act of assigning language to describe Oneness automatically creates a subject and an object, which equals two. I think Tony Parsons puts it best when he says, "It is not a door, it is God dooring." I do my best to communicate that which cannot be put into words. I encourage you not to be concerned with the words and just come to the party. Sit back, relax, and trust that this will get you nowhere.

In April 2003 in Brussels, I had what I now refer to as a "glimpse." Maybe you've had a similar experience. One minute I was fishing around in the trunk of the car and the next I felt as though my heart were exploding. The scenery glimmered briefly and reappeared just as before, yet radically different. Everything was Love: the ant on the sidewalk, the child on the sidewalk, the sidewalk in itself: all love.

As I sat with my clients that Spring day, I kept grabbing my chair, because it felt that my body was passing through it. It was clear that there was no separation between any person, object, or myself. "We are all One" was no longer a concept. As I listened to my clients speak of their struggles, I could never find a problem. Every sound was met with complete acceptance. We shared a lot of laughter that day. When there is no resistance to life exactly as it is, there is no longer anything to fight against! Instead of seeing my clients as needing healing, I saw them as we all are: whole and complete. How could anything possibly be missing or need changing when everything is love? The only odd thing was that I hadn't realized this sooner. It was so normal, that it seemed impossible to live any other way. This perspective lasted three weeks, and then started bobbing in and out for the next three months. After four months I was panicking; where did it go and how could I get it back?

Up until this occurrence, I believed that events happened sequentially and that one thing led to another, as a line of dominos logically knocks the next one down. I believed that I was living my life, on a path, and getting better all of the time. Before the glimpse, I didn't understand sayings such as, "Life is just an illusion," "This is all just a dream," and "It's a holographic Universe and everything exists simultaneously." Then, suddenly, life was living itself and there was no me controlling it (as if I ever had!). (Don't fret, this cannot be understood by the mind, so don't even bother.)

After that fourth month, I judged every experience as inferior to that initial glimpse, which left me feeling dry and lost. I judged my personality as a sham and didn't know how to relate to life. My marriage dissolved, I moved back to the United States, and I felt conflicted about seeing healing clients. I didn't want to feed the suffering that comes from believing that it is possible to be separate from the Universe. I still don't.

It is now April 2005. Many times over the past two years, being able to see with the perspective of Oneness has arisen and fallen like the tide. I have struggled in frustration trying to hold onto it. I have raged against the Personality. What I now know is that in the eyes of God, it is all equal. God is now experiencing frustration - Great! God is now experiencing awareness—Great! God is now experiencing grief - Great! There is no judgment, no experience better than another. My mind doesn't agree with that, as it is busy doing its job of viewing life with the perspective of "twoness." I no longer expect my mind to do something it was not made to do.

My personality and all of its quirks exists within the Oneness. I have preferences and want certain outcomes, and from this perspective things happen sequentially. I can argue with life and suffer, and that is okay. I can feel grateful and open my eyes in awe to the mystery of life and celebrate all that I am, and that is okay.

I've made peace with seeing clients. I do it now for sharing in the joy of awareness dawning, which is an honor that I don't want to miss. Life is to be experienced as it is, on its own terms. You can be grateful for that or not. Gratefulness offers a certain perspective and therefore experience of life in that moment. Give it a try sometime.

℀ Elizabeth Menzel

Let's Show Our Gratitude to Our Seniors

Kay Presto

*T*he saying on the elderly man's T-shirt startled me. It read: "I'm a cranky old Grandpa!" "Did he buy that for himself?" I wondered, "or did his family give that to him?" That negative message certainly had me puzzled. The seniors I know, from their 50s to those in their 90s, don't have that negative kind of attitude. They're busy volunteering, repairing toys for children, assisting police departments, delivering Meals on Wheels, and so much more. A few days later, I saw an older woman wearing a T-shirt that showed a lady slumped over in her rocking chair, with the saying, "I'm an old Grandma in a rocking chair." <u>Another</u> negative message! That puzzled me even more.

Were there <u>positive</u> messages out there for seniors? Determined to find out, I went to a national T-shirt show, and sadly discovered that all their senior shirts had only negative messages. By then, I was truly frustrated. I felt that America's hard-working men and women who had helped build this country, who had gone through wars to protect us, deserved better than that. *How* could we honor them? While driving home, my mind was churning with ideas.

When I arrived home, I told my husband, "You'll wonder why I'm doing this, but I'm going to start a T-shirt company." With disbelief, he said, "You're already covering auto racing, you're writing, and you're a professional speaker; where do you plan to find the time?" I didn't know, but was resolved to try.

My first phone call was to Marilyn Anderson, a great professional artist who has done work for me. I told her, "I want a T-shirt design that's colorful and energetic, and that says: 'I'M A SENSATIONAL SENIOR!' She went to work on several, and her third design was exactly what I had visualized.

Soon I was immersed in copyrighting it and finding a good screenprinting company. Luckily, my son and his wife had already reviewed companies for their own T-shirt business. That saved me time, but I quickly found out that this new business required inventory control, sales tax, a state selling number, and much more. It was an entire new world for me. My husband and I began selling the shirts at Business Expo's, Senior Expo's, and Christmas Fairs. Now we've added a Web site.

Seniors began to ask for V-neck shirts. We added those to our inventory. Then we had calls for sweatshirts. We soon added those, along with mugs, and other items are currently being planned.

The "Sensational Senior!" merchandise is now being sold around the country, worn proudly by men and women just turning 50 to those in their late 90s. This positive movement to honor seniors *is* growing. Greg Reid, author of the best-selling book *The Millionaire Mento*r, is my brilliant mentor. He suggested sending these shirts to celebrities, so that's what I did. Legendary singer Pat Boone certainly likes his. "I think your 'Sensational Seniors!' movement is a terrific idea," he wrote to me, "and I vouch for the vigor, vitality, and creativity of today's seniors." He is so right, and Pat is a perfect example of a senior who is living life to its fullest and best.

As I search, I find more inspiring examples. Despite her back problems, a 92-year-old woman cleans her own house, volunteers in a nearby hospital gift shop, and drives to the Senior Center in her town, not to eat, but to serve lunches to seniors much younger than she! Others knit caps, booties, and coverlets for children's hospitals. If their bodies don't work well, their fingers still do. I've seen partially disabled men climbing on the roofs of Habitat for Humanity houses, lovingly building homes for those in need.

In tribute to our veterans, volunteers, and seniors of all ages, I say "My hat's off to you; you're all 'Sensational Seniors!'"

Am I grateful for all the extra work this new business has created? I truly am, and I'm grateful that I originally saw those T-shirts with such a sad message. I'm grateful that God inspired me to add this entire new dimension to my life. I'm glad that He planted this seed to encourage us to respect our seniors and pay tribute to them for all their hard work and sacrifice. They deserve our gratitude, not our disdain.

It is my fervent wish that we create "I'm A Sensational Senior!" clubs all through this wonderful country of ours, with every member wearing these T-shirts bearing this proud message. I hope that this

Wake up... Live the Life You Love, Giving Gratitude

movement will instill in our nation the pride, and caring, toward our seniors that they so justly deserve.

I'm planning to write a series of books filled with stories about our wonderful seniors, and as a former talk-show host, to begin a new television show to bring their remarkable stories to the viewing world. Yes, America, our seniors are definitely "Sensational!" I'm truly proud—and extremely grateful—that we can pay tribute to them.

ભ Kay Presto

Gratitude Means So Very Much to Me

Domingo Ivan Casañas

*T*hanksgiving, gratitude, and being grateful...those are such powerful words, simple to say, simple to read, simple to write. However, many of us are too busy or are too rushed to put these words into action. To me, these words are precious because I am so grateful for the freedoms that I have in this country, the United States of America. You see, I was born in Cuba, where freedom no longer exists.

Would our world be different today if everyone were to give thanks, show gratitude, and be grateful for what they have? Would the world be a more pleasant place, if we were to be polite and give thanks for what others do for us? Could we feel inspired listening to others give praise and thanks to our Creator? If we showed gratitude for what we should be thankful for, would our world have stronger morals instead of experiencing moral decay?

I truly believe that the answer to all these questions would be YES! If we would show gratitude our world would be a better place. It is never too late. A chain reaction could start and we would soon experience the positive effects of gratitude all over the world.

In March 2004, I came close to dying during a five-by-pass open heart surgery. I was afraid that I would not be there for my children. I am the single father of three great teenagers. I am so thankful to God for them. They are the joy of my life. Since March 2004, I am more thankful than ever for being able to share my life with them. My thankfulness to my Savior Jesus Christ is so powerful and I know that He feels my gratitude for being alive and healthy.

We should not wait for a near-death situation before we are thankful for our lives. Instead, being grateful—and showing it— should become a daily habit for us all. Think about it; we have so much to be grateful for. Get a pen and paper and start making a list of what you are grateful for. You will see that things that you don't usually think about will start appearing. Praise God for what you have, instead of constantly asking for more. Your act of gratitude will be rewarded and others around you will know that you are truly blessed. As you spend another day in your life, show thanksgiving to others. Show them that you are smiling because you are grateful to be alive, and your example will help others.

My prayer for all of us, right now, is to have a spirit of thankfulness in our hearts. Don't be afraid to show it. Be grateful for your freedom, your relationship with Jesus Christ, your children, your home, your job, the love you feel, your material possessions, your marriage, your health, your family, and your surroundings. I pray also for those who may be missing some of these things.

We can all make a difference in the lives of others if we show that we appreciate them, that we care about them and that we are grateful for them. I give you my sincere appreciation for allowing me to share with you how I feel about giving thanks, and being grateful. You, too, can start on this same path of gratitude. Once you start, your gratitude will make others feel better about you and about themselves. May God bless you!

ᔕ Domingo Ivan Casañas

Gratitude Essay
Todd Bramson

I have gained wisdom, strength of character, integrity, empathy, and the value of giving by my parents' example. Unfortunately, my father passed away very suddenly at the age of 45, when I was just 16. It was less than three weeks from the day he discovered a few black and blue marks on his arms until the day he died of acute leukemia. In this short time, we never had a chance to talk about the future, although I feel his guidance through my conscience and in the wisdom of others, including my mother.

It is interesting how the experiences of childhood, both good and bad, mold the path we follow as adults. My dad did not have much life insurance, or any established relationships with trusted advisors. When he died, my mother was lost financially. She was given very poor financial advice and the modest life insurance proceeds were lost in an unsuitable and inappropriate investment. My family's misfortune defined my passion. It was through this unfortunate situation that I became empowered. My mission has remained intact for over 25 years: I decided this would never happen to my family or anyone who entrusted me with their important financial decisions.

Because of our significant financial crisis I became eligible for an Evans Scholarship. In the early 1930's, Chick Evans became a nationally ranked golfer and started a college scholarship program with his earnings. This scholarship has now grown to the largest privately funded scholarship in the country. There are over 820 students currently benefiting from it and more than 8,000 alumni. His vision and generosity have been an inspiration to me.

With that in mind, I started Bramson and Associates, LLC. This company is founded with the following mission:

First, I wanted to honor my family. Before he passed away, my dad started an advertising company named Bramson and Associates. Now, I can carry on the name and continue his vision of helping people. In addition, I can involve my family in the business as he intended to do with me.

Second, I want to bring significant value in the form of:
- entertaining and informative seminars, workshops and speeches
- valuable monthly emails with cutting edge ideas
- books and resources that provide valuable wisdom
- an efficient, useful website that includes links to sites that are important and valuable

Third, I want to promote the spirit of generously "giving something back." As Bramson and Associates, LLC grows, I intend to model the philanthropic vision that Chick Evans started over seventy years ago.

I'd like to share a proverb containing some valuable wisdom and insight:

He (or She!) who knows, and knows he knows, is wise;
Follow him (her).

He who knows, but knows not that he knows, is asleep;
Awaken him.

He who knows not, and knows he does not know, is simple;
Teach him.

He who knows not, but does not know that he knows not, is dangerous;
Avoid him.

I believe it's our mission in life to listen to and learn from, or **follow** those who fall into the first category. It is also our mission to take our unique gifts and make them available to those who are asleep or simple by **awakening** and **teaching** them. Also, time is too precious to spend with those who are dangerous, so **avoid** and minimize the amount of time you spend with people who fall into this category, and your enjoyment of life will multiply. We all have unique gifts and abilities and to the extent that our lives overlap and intertwine, we can all grow together carrying out our unique visions.

 co Todd D. Bramson

A Celebration of Life:
Living With a Heart of Gratitude!!
Michael Adul'Ali

Dana looked around the church, taken aback by the number of people there to celebrate the life of her husband and to grieve his loss. Hundreds of chairs lined the lawn outside the church as the church pews filled and the mourners spilled outside. Loudspeakers were set up. Policemen directed traffic. It was surreal.

A flash fire at the chemical plant where he was working took Will's life. Twenty-three hours of suffering with third-degree burns on 98 percent of his body was an unfitting end for a young man who was well-respected, well-liked, and deeply loved. He was a husband, a father, a co-worker, and a softball teammate. He adored Dana and his girls. "I love you, I'll see you in Heaven," were the last words that he spoke to them.

Walking down the center aisle holding the hands of her daughters, Jo and Aubri, Dana didn't feel the weight of grief. She felt the comfort of grace. And she felt thankful. Her gratitude had nothing to do with her loss and had everything to do with her faith.

"In everything give thanks for this is the will of God in Christ Jesus concerning you."

The verse from I Thessalonians 5 ran through her mind.

"In everything," she thought. "Not for everything." Dana offered up a silent prayer of thanksgiving.

Jo crawled into Dana's lap and fell asleep as Aubri played with her aunt's jewelry. At five and seven-years old, they didn't have a real grasp yet of what was ahead. But then again, neither did Dana.

Choices: living a life of gratitude involves *choosing* to live a life of gratitude. Does gratitude come naturally or do we have to conscientiously choose to be filled with thankfulness and appreciation? Sheldon Kopp provides us with this insight: *"Life can be counted on to provide all the pain that any of us might need."* While our circumstances are often out of our control, our reaction to them is not.

Christine awoke, once again, in excruciating pain. Her lupus was debilitating and the pain was robbing her of her desire to live. With two young daughters of her own, she faced certain pain and discouragement every day. She wanted to be an attentive and caring wife and mother. Instead, for months Christine saw herself simply as a burden to her family.

But today was different. No, the pain hadn't lessened. The lupus wasn't gone. The path was long, arduous, and disheartening. But Christine woke up this morning grateful for another day to spend with her family. As she struggled out of bed, she softly sung the words of her favorite Maranatha song:

> *In His time,*
> *In His time,*
> *He makes all things beautiful*
> *In His time...*

How could she sing of beauty when her own body was twisted in pain? Where does someone like Christine, or like her friend, Dana, find joy within their circumstances?

Where is the bitterness or the anger?

Living a life of gratitude doesn't mean that you don't experience anger, sadness, or even bitterness. It means that, despite everything, no matter how you feel, no matter what your circumstances may be, no matter what, you still choose to be grateful.

Gratitude must be cultivated and practiced. Sometimes it's hard work developing an attitude of gratitude but the benefits are worth it! When we express our gratitude, we rise above our circumstances. We acknowledge that there is always something to be thankful for and that there is something greater than our problems on which we should focus.

For Christine, it is as simple as, "I can't get out of bed today, but I'm grateful that my eyes can focus on the beauty of my children's faces." Her choices are to focus on her pain and suffering or to rise above them and truly see something good.

Dana faces choices everyday. Her husband is dead; that's a fact. In the months following his death, she was burdened with betrayal from his family, her lawyer, the company that her husband worked for, and others. Will's life insurance policy was given to his parents. State laws prevented her from bringing a lawsuit against the com-

Wake up... Live the Life You Love, Giving Gratitude

pany responsible for his death, so she was left without a settlement. Unfortunately, the list goes on and on.

Dana has every right to feel bitter toward life and the hand that it's dealt her. No one would blame her. No one would be surprised. But what would a life of bitterness accomplish for her? Chances are slim that Dana, or anyone else consumed in bitterness, would have a chance at happiness if the choice was made to wallow in self-pity or remorse. Of course, Dana experienced anger. She felt betrayed. She felt frightened. Her emotions ran the gamut, which was understandable; they needed to. The natural cycle of grief, whether you lose a loved one, a job, the use of your legs, or a marriage, has to be worked out. But you can work through your grief with a spirit of thankfulness.

The benefits of a life of gratitude include feelings of peacefulness, joy, serenity, and optimism. There is power in choosing one's attitude. It's the kind of power that gives you the confidence that you can make it through anything that is thrown your way. The joy that you feel becomes your strength. You can rise each morning looking forward to the experiences ahead, rather than pulling up the covers and wallowing in your own world of disappointment, loss, pain, and disillusionment. You have a choice! That fact, in and of itself, is a reason for celebration! Try on some gratitude today. You'll be amazed at how good you look!

ల Michael Adul'Ali

Wake up... Live the Life You Love, Giving Gratitude

Change That Chose Me
Colin Smith

I was born on July 25th, 1935, the seventh child in a close farm family of nine children. Being the youngest son (and left-handed), I worked hard on the family farm so we could produce and to enjoy our abundant crops. But, on my first day of school, I sat with my head down, not speaking a word.

Yet, I was a very curious boy. I like to read, to learn and the challenge myself daily. At six, I felt that other people and things were more important than I was, and decided to make my own way along.

I returned home after two years of high school. A few years later, when our father died, I took on more responsibility. In the midst of my newfound responsibility, my youngest sister married. It was this marriage that sparked the belief that it was time for me to do something for myself, and the family farm was sold. I worked in rural land development until I drew an irrigation block in a ballot of a government sponsored irrigation scheme.

A Blessing in Disguise!

Ten years later, a government official set out to collect overdue water charges. After an interview, I sought medication for traumatic shock and disbelief, which graduated to unexpressed anger, anxiety and depression: an unexplained "mental block" had settled on me. Five years later, I decided it was time to salvage the situation, and to get away from it all. I began to study the concepts of Permaculture.

Everything Happens for The Best:

Eleven years after the mental block began, I experienced another panic attack, and, oddly, felt relieved. It had been only two months before that I had bought Stephen Covey's Handbook, *Daily Reflections for Highly Effective People*. After the attack, I sought help from a psychologist, who primed me for a two week admission to a Hospital Live-in Group Cognitive Therapy Program.

When I knew the date of my admission, I read the Daily Reflection for June 2nd, 1996, which read: "Whether we are aware of it or not, whether we are in control of it or not, there is a first creation to every part of our lives. We are either the second creation of our own proactive design, or we are the second creation of other peoples' agendas, of circumstances, or of past habits."

Inspired, I turned to The Daily Reflection for June 3rd, and read: "I can change. I can live out of my imagination, instead of my memory. I can tie myself to my limitless potential instead of my limiting past. I can become my own first creator."

Right On Cue

I recognized the significance of these Daily Reflections, and showed them to my psychologist and the hospital psychiatrist. Both responded, "How prophetic!"

Three weeks after the program concluded, and just before a "Refresher Weekend," I attended a Louise Hay "You Can Heal Your Life Weekend Workshop." It came into my life "right on cue." I lost my anxiety, my Emotional Quotient rose, lifting my Intelligence Quotient, and my values changed.

"And the day came when the risk to remain tight in the bud becomes more painful than the risk to bloom"-Anias Nin.

I now know I inherited an aberration from my mother. From a recent personality check, I recognize the thoroughness of my father, and the creativity of my mother. These traits helped shaped me into the person I am today once I was able to add my own creative contribution.

On the first day of the International Permaculture Conference in Perth, the Daily Reflection for September 28th, 1996, said: "A tendency that has run through your family for generations can stop with you. You're a transition person—a link between the past and the future. And your own change can affect many, many lives downstream. You can write it in your personal mission statement and into your mind and heart. You can visualise yourself living in harmony with that mission statement in Your Daily Private Victory."

An Opportunity to Change

The crisis enabled me to grow and change. I now challenge myself to be "The World I Want to See." I now live a life of enjoyment grounded in my creativity. I have a strong, melodious voice, and learned to recite "Desiderata," and I plan to recite it for release soon.

Wake up... Live the Life You Love, Giving Gratitude

I am also writing a book, giving it the outrageous title, "*Why Kangaroos - And Other Dumb Creatures-Don't Have Hospitals!*" It is a send up of the "Band-Aids on Band-Aids" approach of the institutionalized health system presently entrenched in western countries.

I am thankful that, even though I did not want to change my life, change chose me.

ɔ Colin Smith

Wake up... Live the Life You Love, Giving Gratitude

Nothing Is As It Seems
Gail Michael

I look back on my blessed life and have such gratitude for where it has taken me. I believe that if I hadn't made it to this place in my life, I would never have understood or appreciated my purpose. Believe me, it was tough going through each experience at the time: the abuse, neglect, loss, abandonment, hunger, and loneliness I felt as a child and throughout my life.

I came into this world born to a mother and father who were so engulfed in the pain in their own lives, trying to make it work for themselves that the last thing they needed was another child. I knew in my heart that each of them loved me as much as they could at the time. The first thing I remembered upon awakening into the realm of this world was the look in my mother's eyes. I saw weariness and fear. I thought I glimpsed love, but I wasn't sure. I'm sure she was thinking, *"How will I take care of another when I am struggling myself?"*

So, I came out of the womb as the "little warrior child." At three years old, I took care of the newest baby in the house, loving him and caring for him. At age four, I experienced sexual abuse, which continued over the next four years. After each encounter, I would try to curl up inside myself, attempting to escape in my dreams, fearful that someone would come and take me back to the bad place. At age four, all I wanted was to die, but the angels and Mary would never allow it. Mary was always with me and, in my small mind, I thought she was evil, for she was the one who always took me back from my dreams. My spirit and my soul were captured and returned to wakefulness and the fear that surrounded me. That was how my little mind remembered it each night.

When I was eleven, I tried to die again, but was stopped by a Great Angel. I turned my anger and rage upon myself. I continued my life of physical illness and pain, torturing myself, creating my own prison, my own hell.

As I grew, I experimented with drugs and alcohol and tried to find love for the wrong reasons, becoming a victim of abuse and poverty. It's amazing the life you can create as an adult, from the pictures you have filed and saved in your mind, both real and embellished by fear. I was lost and deeply depressed for years, until the mother I never really knew, or had the opportunity to love, was diagnosed with cancer. I believe that those with long terminal illnesses are angels who linger here in that state of illness with their undying love to assist us, until we can finally see what we came here to learn.

In that last year of my mother's life, I learned who she was as a mother, a friend, and a human being. I learned that she was very well-loved by others in town where I grew up.

In her last year, we dropped our ego masks that we had carried through our lives and we faced each other with open hearts. We began to love so deeply that we got lost in that love and created a space in time in which everything was healed through all eternity—past, present, and future. It was the most profound thing I have ever experienced.

My mother showed me who she was and who I was. I found her that last year, the mother I never knew, and she left me so filled with her. I have felt her inside me since her death, and all around me, as if she had never left. I still carry her with me everywhere, and oftentimes, I catch a whiff of her scent. I feel her arms around me, and hear her voice telling me she loves me and that she is proud of me. Sometimes, I even feel that I am she and she is me.

I truly believe that those who have hurt me, the pain of my life, and the debilitating disease I created in my forties, were all precious gifts to show me *self-love*. If I had not experienced any of these things and instead had a mother and father holding my hand along the way, loving and supporting me, I would never have come to learn *forgiveness* and self-love; and I would never have seen the light that I am.

So, the greatest gift that I have received in this lifetime is the gift that my mother gave me. She dedicated her life to me, to show me who I was. I know it was as painful for her as it was for me, and thank God for the veils that protect us when we need to be numbed for a bit. I have no judgment on any of it, for it all served a larger purpose that I now understand.

Wake up... Live the Life You Love, Giving Gratitude

Our lives are nothing but a journey to show us ourselves in the mirror and to teach us about love of self. We are the light. We are love. If we could only get past the mind more quickly and see that everything serves a purpose, if we could only forgive all others for everything we perceive they are doing to us, and if we could only forgive ourselves, we would be able to see more clearly and love so deeply all those who come before us to assist us along the way. How incredible is my gratitude for all those who have come to assist me!

ᏉᎬ Gail Michael

Taking the Plunge

Brian Yui

They say the first time is always the hardest: first time at bat, first date, first time jumping off the high-dive. We fear failure, or success, but most of all, we are afraid of committing to the unknown.

I was a commercial real estate executive. Every day, I went to work in a suit and tie, briefcase in hand, and my secret ambitions tucked out of sight. It was a respectable job, but I yearned for something more. From the time I was a teenager, I had quietly nurtured my entrepreneurial drive. Slowly, I began investing in real estate, buying as many fixer-uppers as I could afford. Within a few years, I had completed 15 transactions. I would buy a house, renovate and sell it, sometimes within a week or two. I kept my day job. I was making money, but the process was nerve-racking. The paperwork was overwhelming, and the realtors involved were making as much, or more, than I was without assuming any of the risk.

It was 1999, and the dotcom craze was at its peak. With my other job as a safety net, I co-founded HouseRebate.com, an online discount real estate brokerage. We offered a one percent rebate to homebuyers and deeply discounted commissions to sellers. I envisioned the company to be a pioneer in real estate like Charles Schwab was in the investment brokerage industry. I was not alone. Discount real estate companies were popping up all over the Internet. As dotcom turned to "dot bomb," our competitors fell victim to the flagging economy. I was afraid we were next, and then, real disaster struck.

We had spent most of working capital on website development and marketing. One day, I tried to log-in, and HouseRebate.com was gone. Gone! It was as if my ambitions and the previous years' work building a business had never existed. After much nail-biting and countless frantic calls, I discovered that our domain name, our storefront, our stock in trade expired. It had been purchased by a man named, Emmet Dalton, and he held the key to my future.

As I contemplated giving up, the phrase, "Out of adversity comes greatness," ran on an endless loop in my head. I made lists, calculated risk-reward, held back, pushed forward, but I never fully committed. Losing the website was the catalyst; I was prepared to quit my day job and pay whatever Emmet asked to take back HouseRebate.com. Fear of the unknown be damned! Holding all the cards, Emmet Dayton (may his karmic savings account always yield interest) asked only that we cover his expenses. For less than $100, I secured my future.

I am happy to report that HouseRebate.com has been profitable since 2002. Living life fully is about swinging for the fences and letting go of your fear. It is finding your purpose and becoming passionate about it. Without the passion, you will never feel the full effect from your purpose in life. So, the next time you tentatively inch out on the high-dive, toes curled over the edge and hanging on for dear life, take a deep breath and take the plunge. Be thankful for the opportunity; it could change your life.

cℕ Brian Yui

Gratitude and the MasterMind:
Thank you, Ben Franklin, Andrew Carnegie and Napoleon Hill
John Dealey

*L*et us begin with a quotation and a request from my dear friend and fellow mastermind enthusiast.

"It's my perfect dream to get every person enrolled in a MasterMind group.

That will make the world

A better,

Safer,

Richer,

Healthier

Happier, and

More meaningful place to live.

From my heart to your heart, please share this. Thank you."

—Mark Victor Hansen

Thankful—Grateful—Gratitude! Oh my! All those words—even all those words together—are not nearly enough to cover the huge debt of gratitude and thankfulness I feel for the marvelous MasterMind work of Andrew Carnegie and Napoleon Hill. It has meant so much to my life and to the lives of many others in my world.

It all started, simply enough, when I fell in love with a lovely woman and we decided to marry. We had a marvelous wedding with lots of friends and family in one of the oldest churches in the South. We danced until dawn; outside under the stars in beautiful May weather.

One night during our honeymoon in the Smoky Mountains, an event in an ice cream store changed our lives forever. Little did we know at the time that it would result in our becoming self-made millionaires over the next couple of years at the very young ages of 27 and 26! We were introduced to a brand new business idea called Earth Shoes. No one at that time had ever heard of them. It sounded so great that we decided to move 1,000 miles from our home in the South to marvelous Minnesota, where we would start a retail location in Minneapolis.

My father listened quietly as we told him about our new opportunity. Then he said, "Hmmm, a new marriage, move far away from home, no job, no friends, no business associates, and start a brand new business?" "Sounds like a mouthful to me!"

I replied, "I don't see what's so hard about all that."

Much to my surprise, HE WAS RIGHT! I didn't find that out for a few months, though.

With all the eagerness, energy, and enthusiasm of youth, we did it. A few months later we had moved, found a rental house and rented a location for the store. We had more inventory delivered to our front door in one day than I thought anybody would need in a lifetime. We were ready to open the store. Suddenly, I saw what my father had seen: a most daunting situation. Just as I was feeling most overwhelmed; I got an invitation to go to a meeting. It was called a MasterMind meeting. It was fashioned along the lines of a group called the Junto, founded by Benjamin Franklin over 200 years ago.

That first meeting I attended was absolutely incredible! The power, the ideas, the energy, the support, the connection, the openness; it was something I had never experienced before! It was amazing.

I didn't say much in the first meeting. However, to myself I said, "I don't know how this group works;

- I don't know what the investment is.
- I don't know what the membership requirements are.
- I don't know or care about any of that.
- There is so much power here, one way or another. I WILL be a part of this group!"

As it turned out, about half of this group were business owners. Through the incredible power and energy that occurs in the MasterMind process, I received invaluable ideas, support, and wisdom about my own business. When I say that I am a self-made millionaire, I should probably say, instead, that I am a "Mastermind-made millionaire."

Over the following ten to fifteen years, I was able to use that power and those principles to help many people and to take many other

Wake up... Live the Life You Love, Giving Gratitude

businesses to success. The principles, support, and relationships built with the MasterMind concepts, can help lead anyone to success.

Despite all the wonderful benefits that can be derived from MasterMind meetings, most people have never even heard of MasterMind. Thankfully, that is changing. The power and influence they can develop is often absolutely incredible: Look at the lasting affect Jesus, Buddha, Andrew Carnegie, and all of their disciples have had on this world.

We would be thankful for the chance to help you learn this powerful principle.

ေ John Dealey

Attitude of Gratitude
Pamela L. Catey, M.A.

Can you list five things for which you are grateful? Being grateful takes practice, and with practice one can become a master. What does being grateful mean to you? With an "Attitude of Gratitude" anything is possible. I'd like to share with you how the practice of giving thanks and being grateful has influenced my life. To find out how it can impact yours will take commitment, action, and practice.

On January 30, 2001, I began the practice of keeping a "Gratitude Journal." My father had been diagnosed with cancer and was about to undergo aggressive chemotherapy treatment. At the time, I was living 1600 miles away from my family and felt compelled to move home and be with them through this challenging time. Once I made the choice to go, everything I needed to handle happened with ease and grace. Within a week of making this resolute decision, I had the support of my husband, a massage therapist to take care my massage therapy practice in my absence, and a massage therapist position waiting for me at a spa 60 miles away from where my parents lived. I remember the first morning waking up in my parents' home and saying to myself: "I am so blessed to be living a life I designed."

During the three months I lived/worked/played in Michigan, I wrote in my gratitude journal everyday. I would write at least five things for which I was grateful. Sometimes they were mundane things like "I am grateful for this comfortable pen to write with." Sometimes it was more serious: "I am grateful for the chemotherapy killing the cancer cells in my father's body." Other times, I would write what I call "Intentional Gratitude Statements." These are statements giving thanks for something (a result, emotive state, object, whatever you desire to create) that does not yet exist in your perception of reality, but which you intend. Thus, you are giving thanks for its arrival into your life. Wallace Wattles speaks directly to the process of intentional gratitude statements in, "*The Science of Getting Rich.*"

There is a thinking stuff from which all things are made, and which, in its original state, permeates, penetrates, and fills the interspaces of the universe.

A thought in this substance produces the thing that is imaged by the thought.

A person can form things in his thought, and by impressing his thought upon formless substance can cause the thing he thinks about to be created.

A person may come into full harmony with the formless substance by entertaining a lively and sincere gratitude for the blessings it bestows upon him. Gratitude unifies the minds of individuals with the intelligence of substance, so that a person's thoughts are received by the formless.

A person can remain upon the creative plane only by uniting himself with the formless intelligence through a deep and continuous feeling of gratitude.

A person must form a clear and definite mental image of the things he wishes to have, to do, or to become, and he must hold this mental image in his thoughts while being deeply grateful to the Supreme that all his desires are granted to him.

You can use this process to create anything you want in your life. Being grateful is the key to creating all that you desire. The practice of being grateful and giving thanks shifts your focus and brings more of what you are focusing on into your life. It opens up your heart and spirit to the magic and miracle of being alive. It also keeps you grounded in reality, present to the reality of your glorious life.

And sometimes, a tragedy truly is a disguised blessing for which you are eternally grateful. My father's cancer forever changed my life. I am grateful for hearing the Wake Up Call that this event was for me. Until that point, I had been living my life as if I had all the time in the world to create my dreams. The lesson I learned from my father's illness is that there is no time like the present to live your dreams. If you are going to work hard (which most of us do), work hard at creating a life you love, work hard at manifesting your dreams, and be grateful for each day. You just don't have all the time in the world to create your dreams; all you have is here and now, and only <u>you</u> get to choose what to do with it. Be grateful for this

Wake up... Live the Life You Love, Giving Gratitude

moment. Be grateful for all you have now. Be grateful for all the good things coming your way.

I invite you today to buy yourself a beautiful journal that you can call your "Gratitude Journal" and keep it next to your bed. Then, every night before you go to sleep, with an "Attitude of Gratitude" write down five things for which you are grateful and one "intentional gratitude statement." Do this for 30 days and let me know your results.

                                             ✎ Pamela L. Catey

Not in My Time, but in Perfect Time
Theresa Burke

*M*y husband and I had been married six years and we had been trying to have a child ever since. I often cried, but my mother always said, "Things do not happen in your time, but they always happen at the perfect time." At the time I didn't understand.

My mother, Diana Esposito, was diagnosed with lung cancer in 1994. I learned that most lung cancer patients do not live more than a year after being diagnosed. I thought, "That is so unfair. A 24-year-old should not have to lose her mother." I prayed and prayed that God would not take her. I was not ready for her to go. God saved her many times. She did not act as if she was in pain and she was in good spirits, even though she knew she had so little time left. I wanted her to know my children, the ones I did not yet have, the ones doctors said I could not have. I knew down deep that one day I would be blessed with a child.

I spent many hours in doctor's offices and hospitals, having blood work done and having tests taken, but it was always the same result. The doctors said that I would never and should never have children. They said that my heart could not handle the pressure and that I could not carry a baby even if I did get pregnant. I chose not to believe them and kept believing that one day I would have children. Then it finally happened. In 1999, I found out that I was pregnant with my son, Joseph.

There would be a new baby in the family. The families were excited, but everyone had hesitations. Would I be able to carry the baby to term? Would my heart be able to handle the stress? Both of my parents were concerned when they heard the news. My mother smiled, but I knew she was afraid for me. I could see the fear in her eyes.

I had the same fears. I was happy and worried at the same time. I wanted my mother to see my baby. At first, things went just as the doctors had said. My body did not want to carry the child. I went to the emergency room thirteen times, in danger of losing my son. Each time the sonogram showed that he was fine. My mother went with me every time she could. We both thought that the sonograms

Wake up... Live the Life You Love, Giving Gratitude

might be the only way she was going to see the baby. I was on bed rest for nearly six months.

On January 13, 2000, my son, Joseph Alexander Burke, was born. My mother was there with me. She was tired and very sick, but she was there. She was the first in my family to see my baby. Against all odds, I had my baby and my mother in the same room.

The doctors said I would never have another child. But that was fine with me. My son was all I wanted. Although it had not happened in my time, it was in perfect time. I needed my son to help me through the last part of my mother's life. He kept my mind off losing her. How could I see this wonderful new creation and be sad at the same time?

My mother loved Joseph. Everything he did was amazing to her. She thought he was the smartest, most wonderful thing on the face of the Earth. She bragged about him to everyone. She was getting weaker by the day, but she never complained. I was so happy that my mother was able to spend time with my son that I completely forgot she was ill.

Then reality hit. Just five days before his first birthday, my son became very ill. I called my mother and told her I was going to take him to the hospital. It was a very short conversation. My mother sounded weak, but at the time I did not notice. I told her that I loved her and would call her later to tell her how Joseph was doing. The doctor said that Joseph was dehydrated, was given intravenous medications and he was fine. I got home early the next morning and spent the day with my son.

Later that evening, while I was feeding my son, my husband walked in. He took Joseph from me and told me to sit down. He had an awful look on his face. He gave me the news that I had been dreading for years now: my mother was gone. I screamed and I cried. I was very angry. How could I live without her?

It was difficult, but Joseph kept me busy. When I was sad about my mother, I would hold him and love him just the way she had loved me. I thought of all the times that he had made her smile and knew why I was not able to have children until I did. There was a purpose. I needed my son to console me in my mother's absence.

Wake up... Live the Life You Love, Giving Gratitude

Not long after my mother's death, I found out that I was pregnant again, with my daughter, Crystal Diane.

The doctors were wrong; I was given two miracles. In the midst of my grief, my time was consumed with a toddler and another pregnancy. I was given children when I needed them most, not when I thought I wanted them. I am so grateful for perfect timing.

ↄ Theresa Burke

Wake up... Live the Life You Love, Giving Gratitude

With Gratitude...

Deedre Diemer

*L*ying in her bed, knees tucked into her chest, clutching her pillow for security, she sobbed. The cry emanated from the depth of her soul. She didn't want to feel this pain ever again. She trembled and couldn't catch her breath, and for one brief fleeting moment she wondered, "What if I just took some sleeping pills to end this pain?" But then through her tears, she had to laugh, "Great; the only thing I have in the house is Tylenol PM and all that would do is give me a groggy hangover tomorrow...the Universe is not supporting me in offing myself."

All the years of personal growth and spiritual seeking hadn't prepared her for this, or so she mused. She knew that once she'd muster the courage to proceed with the divorce that there would be moments like this: extreme loneliness, self-doubt, grief, and fear; but she also knew it was the cry of her soul to free herself from a once-loving but now destructive, unhealthy, and abusive relationship. "I hate alcohol, and I especially hate cocaine," she muttered to herself. "Dammit! All of our dreams, our hopes, and aspirations gone because of those wretched poisons!" She was filled with rage and fear. "Oh, please dear God, help me! And please send your angels to protect and love him...he's in so much pain! Please help me make it through this dark, lonely night. I know in the light of day, I'll feel better again. Please guide me!"

Then doing what she usually did when she needed some divine guidance, she reached for her Angel Messenger Cards. "Blessings" is the card she picked. Present challenge: seeing the blessings in your life. "No, kidding," she sighed. Have you ever wondered what allows someone to have a thankful heart? What would it be like if you acknowledged the blessing offered you through every relationship and unfolding circumstance? These were the words she read. "Wow...okay, this is a tad challenging at the moment, but I know in my heart that I have a lot to be thankful for." She started with what was immediately in front of her. "I'm grateful for my bed...I'm grateful for my beautiful house...I'm so grateful for my cat...and I'm grateful to my husband." She sobbed as she reflected on all the blessings they had given each other over the past 11 years, even the

Wake up... Live the Life You Love, *Giving Gratitude*

painful ones. She realized that the painful ones had provided her with the opportunity to grow, to gain greater compassion for herself and others. She no longer "judged" those who lost themselves in relationships or remained in one when it was obvious to everyone around how detrimental the relationship had become. She now had compassion for those who couldn't break free from addictions, whether physical, emotional, or mental and she had even greater respect for those who did.

She reflected on their life together and all the beautiful angels that arrived to share her journey: "Dear God, I am so thankful for my wonderful friends who've loved me through all of this. Thank you for my dear friend, Rick, and his family, for being my champion when I'd lost sight of myself. Thank you for Paul, for all the deep talks and words of encouragement at the leg press machine when we were supposed to be working out. Thank you for Traci, who recognized that I was in denial, but who just loved me anyway, waiting for me to wake up. Thank you for Lynn, whose loving expertise has guided me over the past three years. She is an angel. Thank you for Joe, my husband's sponsor, who is truly a gift and a miracle. Thank you for my family, for the opportunity to heal with them as I've gone through this chapter in my life. I am so grateful; thank you for Celia, Mindy, Stephanie, Jack and...."

Her heart seemed to expand with each thought of gratitude, the warmth filling her body. As she focused on what she was grateful for, her fears and anxieties subsided, replaced by peace, serenity, and a knowingness that everything was going to be okay; better than okay. She slept a very deep and healing sleep that night. When she awoke the next morning, with her beloved cat by her side, she felt as if she had been cradled all night long. She breathed a prayer. "Thank you for this beautiful day, for this opportunity and, thank you for reminding me of all that I have to be grateful for. I'm alive, right here, right now and I have a grateful, loving heart!"

When you get caught up in the struggles of day-to-day living, I encourage you to take a moment to reflect upon all that you have to be grateful for. You may be surprised to discover how abundant your life truly is.

లు Deedre Diemer

Grateful for the Bad Times

Dr. R. Winn Henderson

The road of life leads us not only through the sunshine, but also through dark shadows of suffering and circumstances that we often do not fully comprehend. Art Martin presents my story in more detail beginning on page 47 in *Recovering Your Lost Self from Adversity.* Things happened in my life that were not right, things that at first I did not understand. I went from having a happy family and a successful medical practice to living through a divorce and losing my wife, daughter, and career. I was falsely accused and imprisoned for a crime I did not commit.

I was placed in a cell and had no recourse but to seek answers from a power greater than my own. I had drifted away from a childhood with a staunch religious upbringing to an adulthood of dealing with life materialistically. I had fallen into a lifestyle where material things were the center of my world. God had been put on the back burner. Making money and accumulating things had become the focus of my attention.

God had other ideas. He wanted my attention. Using pain and suffering as the catalyst, He got me to fully focus on why He created me. I know it's hard for you to understand why I say, "I am grateful for all of the horrible things that happened to me," but in all candor, I am.

I graduated from high school at age 16 and college at 19. I was the youngest person to graduate from my medical school at 23. Expectations and pressure to excel were great. I got caught up in a life of overachieving to the point of it almost taking over my life. The disruption in 1990 may have saved my life, because I was working too hard at keeping the status quo. At the rate I was going I could have easily died of a heart attack or a stroke. The body can only do so much. I was working up to 20 hours a day seeing patients and keeping up with all the paperwork.

There was an empty hole in my life, which I tried to fill with what was readily available. I had enough money coming in to have a very good life, but it constantly required more as time went on, to pay for

Wake up... Live the Life You Love, Giving Gratitude

all the toys. So God stepped in and grabbed my attention by taking my toys away. A child will cry when he loses his toys, as an adult, I also did some crying because my toys had become such a part of my life.

I know that you are expecting some dramatic ending to this sorrowful tale. I found myself in prison with only 13 items to my name, but I can truthfully say that I was happier at that time than I had ever been. In the quietness of my cell I reached out in my desperation to God, whom I had put on the back burner so many years before. He gave me the answers I needed and made me three unlikely promises, which He subsequently kept. For my part, I started pursuing the mission He revealed to me. I continue to this day trying to fulfill the purpose of my life. This is the reason for my internal joy, happiness, and peace of mind.

You can bet your bottom dollar I am grateful for all the things that have happened to me. I am grateful for both the good and the bad. Without each and every one of these things in my life, I would not be the person I am today. I would not be doing what I am doing today. As I look back on my life, I can say that the happiest time was the night God revealed my mission and put a purpose in my life. He took all the gifts He had given me, my intellect, my training, and my ability to get things done, and He put them to work doing exactly what He originally had in mind for me to do. God gets our attention one way or another.

In telling you this story I am able to pursue my mission, for my mission is to help you find yours. My life is not free from limitations these days, but despite the limitations society has imposed, I will continue daily to do everything in my power to spread this message for as long as I have breath. In this way, I may complete my life's work. I put my faith in God's wisdom and let the message resonate in the lives of others in whatever manner He desires.

If you have a void or emptiness that you want to fill, I would be happy to help you find purpose in your life. My mission is to help you find yours.

ભ Dr. R. Winn Henderson

Wake up... Live the Life You Love, Giving Gratitude

Three Fathers
Robert Valentine

*A*n ancient adage says, "A man may have a hundred fathers, but only one mother."

Without admitting the number, I think there is something in the claim. I can easily recognize three "fathers" who served as guides, inspirations, role models and sources of pride, encouragement and faith. Around the perimeter of that tiny band is a larger crowd of employers, teachers, neighbors and friends who performed similar tasks of kindness. I think most people have a similar count and, if we are wise, we are grateful to them all.

The late William Donald Valentine is, according to official records, deceased. Yet, I find myself having chats with him when I'm alone in my car. I hear his voice, at the oddest times, reciting the old Scottish sayings he would use for advice from time to time. For the balance of my lifetime, I am fairly confident that the late Mr. Valentine will be—for all intents and purposes—immortal.

I seem to have his big hands, his long narrow feet, and the inability to say the name "Charlie" without making it sound like "chah-lee." I've tried, but after forty years of hearing him pronounce it so, I'm stuck.

I inherited his love for words and the power of human speech. I am thankful for his reverence of family and for his abhorrence of political or religious arguments, which accomplish nothing and threaten friendships. No day passes without his example or his teaching influencing what I do, and no one has had a greater effect on me except for his "good wife," my mother.

But I did not go into his business; I went in another direction often led by another man. He is, in a way, a second father.

Dr. Gifford Blyton had an influence on me that was just as important as that of my own father. He had the same influence over dozens—if not hundreds—of young men and women who studied with him at the university. He was enormously successful at winning trophies and accolades, but he was even more successful in teaching honor, common sense, hard work and the value of friendship.

Following his example, I have a tendency to refer to a silly person as a "ned," and to exhort students or co-workers to action with Doc's signature remark: "Let's stop standing around!"

He never "stood around," and was always involved in public and professional service. He is a powerful example to me of how a man ought to behave in my business. When I am in doubt, his lesson points the way.

Some years after my Dad passed away, I had an opportunity to meet another Scotsman. Tom Murray passed through town and, by accident, we met. Since that time, Tom has been like a member of my family.

Like a father, he has filled in the blanks in my history left by too many missed conversations with Dad. At a time in my life when I long to know who I am and from whence I came, he has amplified the stories heard in my boyhood, and added to them. He has kept me from losing touch with my heritage, as so often befalls the first generation Americans. In his genial concern for me and mine, and in his willingness to share his own family, heritage and history, he is another father who has changed my life for the better.

So, on the next Fathers' Day, you might want to consider all the "fathers" who have helped you along the way. I doubt anyone will take offense if I observe that some very good "fathers" have been women—and some have been mothers.

He (or she) need not be connected by blood or kin, but he might be the most important guide you will ever encounter. He is not put there to replace anyone in your life, but to add to the bounty of human influence that helps us grow and makes us better.

Send him a card or, better still, give him a call. His voice is important in your life and it will not hurt you to hear it again.

Tell him, "Thanks."

ↄ Robert Valentine

Embrace Your Daily Gratitude Attitude
Cappi Pidwell

I am grateful for this book, that it exists and that I get to be a part of it! I could go on and on about the things for which I am grateful in my own life, but I want to share how you can transform your life and increase your "Gratitude Energy." It can be activated easily if we consciously practice it every day. It is an extremely powerful energy. I truly believe it is the secret to success in life and the key to getting what you truly desire; it's all based in **Gratitude.**

Most people know it's important to be thankful; to appreciate others and acknowledge the wonderful things we have in our lives. Yet how much of the time do we focus on it and *really feel it*? How many times in a day do we send gratitude out into the universe or appreciate the wonderful things that are enhancing our lives? It could be gratitude for the dry cleaners and your freshly pressed clothes as you put them on in the morning. It could be for your car starting and getting you to your destination or it could be for your phone, connecting you with anyone at your convenience. It can be for thousands of things a day. We have so much at our fingertips, yet most of the time we think only about all the things we don't have.

It seems as though we appreciate things only after something devastating happens, such as a tsunami, or an earthquake or something as devastating as 9-11. Why does it take something shocking for us to open up and be grateful for our families and our lives? Why do we slowly—but—surely go back to life as usual and lose our gratitude and appreciation for all the blessings that surround us.

If everyone were to focus their energies on their gratitude for 10 to 15 minutes a day, what do you think our universe would be like? The universe is so generous and abundant; it gives us everything and anything we desire! Gratitude energy and focus brings **more** to be grateful about and expands that energy out into the universe. It starts with you and me.

The next time you are stressed or struggling with an issue, stop and look around at your immediate environment and really appreciate everything that is surrounding you. I wake up every morning and pick one thing for which I am grateful. I call it my "**daily gratitude**

attitude." If I get into negative thoughts or get stressed out during the day, I think of that one thing I chose that morning and I focus all my energy on it for a few minutes.

You should try my method. Get creative and pick something new everyday. Stick with the same ***daily gratitude attitude*** for the entire day and watch your life expand in ways you never thought possible!! Start to notice more and more of the conveniences you have available to you by opening this energy. You will open up your direct connection with your source and immediately feel better. Let the appreciation and gratitude overflow. Let it fill your cells, your organs, and thoughts. Then go back to your day and notice how different you feel.

The daily gratitude attitude is such a powerful tool. It is something you should practice *every day*. It will then become a natural way of being for you. Gratitude can turn a bad mood into a joyous one; it can make us enjoy life more, as our hearts open to increased appreciation of all that surrounds us. It doesn't take much effort, just willingness and focus. I promise it will support you at every level and your life will be more complete, loving, and fulfilled. Thank yourself and the universe every day for all that you have! Be grateful!

ↂ Cappi Pidwell

Parenting Dad

Lance Shaw

"*K*im, you don't belong to me. You belong to God who loaned you to me for us to mutually influence each other." (I was moving my hand back and forth from her to me.) "This is not a one-way street, and I'm really excited that God picked me for you!" Kim was 3. Her brother, Lance, age 4 ½, got the same message.

Long before Kim and Lance could understand my words, I read to them Dr. Seuss and *Business Week*, both with animated voice inflections. I would say "Lance (or Kim), I earn my living with pencils, paper, and ideas. I'm sure you will too. I want you to become very comfortable with pencils, paper, and ideas." When my marriage ended, I got physical custody of the kids for the first two years. I enrolled them in preschool before Lance turned 5.

I told my children with great sincerity, "Guys, I want to be a loving dad. I'm studying hard and really trying; however, I need your help." I listened to them, especially during unstructured play and in the car during commutes on long trips to visit their mom every other weekend in Sacramento. As I observed the way they parented, I learned a lot.

My children and I were developing a number of fun, creative learning games designed to develop and refine our life philosophies, self-confidence, assertiveness, and compassion. For instance, the kids selected our produce at the supermarket every week. I would say, "Kim, please go get us four to five stalks of celery. Lance, we'll want about five pounds of carrots. When you guys are done with that, get 25 to 30 Granny Smith apples and 25 to 30 bananas." By allowing the kids to select the produce and praising their selections, I was able to convey to them that they had good judgment. This was but one weekly opportunity to reinforce that truth.

Each weekday morning, after a nutritious breakfast, I opened "Dad's Deli" and made our lunches, which included a lunch and a dinner salad in Ziploc bags. I would make comments on the produce. "Kim, you've got to be the best celery picker in all of San Jose!

Lance, these are terrific carrots. And always, guys, Granny Smiths are 'the apples that bite back!'"

Before I became a single dad, I had worked for several Fortune 500 companies: GE (three separate divisions), IBM, Motorola, and FMC. I had developed effective work teams as a department manager and as a project manager. Linking individual rewards and celebrations with team members is crucial in long-term effective team development. "The way we treat people" discussions had so much in common whether on the playground or in the office. I discovered many common threads in effective business leadership and in effective parenting.

I had been project manager for a group of managers of extremely bright engineers, scientists, and business innovators who were developing high tech semiconductor wafer processes and equipment. It was my practice to take my kids in to work sometimes to show what I had explained about how "we" earned money. I wanted them to know they were as critical to my success as I was to theirs.

One of my very first lecturettes when we became a household of three was this, "Guys, in this household, we are absolutely, totally, and completely equal. Just because I'm taller, I don't get any special privileges. However, my role is to be the Parent." After a few months of parenting, I revised the lecturette one Tuesday. "Hey guys, I'm tired of being Parent all the time; Kim, you'll be Parent on Wednesday and Lance, you'll be Parent on Thursday. I'll be Parent on Friday." I folded my arms and smugly continued, "I want to be parent only every third day." I delegated and we negotiated the roles and guidelines for the Parent. I told them that we three had Learner's Permits.

The Parent selected such things as the color-coded route to preschool and where I would go at day's end to eat. He or she would recommend discipline for inappropriate behaviors and other important decisions. I defined discipline as an act of love, and they were allowed to discipline me. They were encouraged to say "no" to me when they disagreed or felt the desire to do so. I encouraged them to be assertive and to say no to me or to anyone when, using their judgment, they felt it was appropriate to do so. I used the same philosophies in my business leadership roles. I did not want to lead people who did not wish to use their judgment.

During our commutes and at home, I often had classical or soft music in the background and either sermons from Peninsula Bible Church or educational, motivational, or inspirational cassette tapes playing. The kids would often critique the tapes. Their favorite author, whom they renamed, was Dr. Wayne Dyer. They'd ask, "Hey dad, would you put on 'Diapers'" (irreverence!). They *did* listen. I adopted one of Dr. Dyer's ideas and wrote "*I LIKE MYSELF*" on a Post-It note and placed it on the mirror where I did "hair-face-and-teeth" time, getting them ready for preschool.

My dad died when I was 4; I don't remember him at all. I wanted my kids and me to mutually influence each other. My prayer at day's end was, "Lord, I wouldn't have missed this day for anything ...z-z-z."

And, my grateful prayer was answered.

                                                ✑ Lance Shaw

The Love Doctor Talks Trash

Mary Gale Hinrichsen, Ph.D.

*L*et's face it: we all strive to be happy, and we all want to be free from the shackles that keep us from moving forward. But where do we start? What steps should we take? Could there be a simple solution?

Over the past ten years of studying human behavior, I have come up with a system that works. Many patients have resolved years of negativity within a few sessions. So I know it is possible to leave hindrances behind, and move toward a great life and future.

Want to know how it's done? It's simple. Just do the following two things:

1. Trash It: Remove all negative barriers that hold us back
2. Become Grateful: Give thanks for what we already have

In all aspects of life, being grateful for what we have is extremely beneficial to our well-being. Of course it's great to want more. In fact, I suggest it. The problem is this: until we first truly appreciate what we have, right now, at this moment, we can not be grateful for future things.

The following two steps will help us to get rid of unwanted trash so we can become grateful for what we have and receive more blessings from God.

Trash is anything that hinders our growth as a person or steals our joy.

STEP 1 - TRASH IT

TRASH MUST BE ACKNOWLEDGED: Know and state what is no longer useful in our lives. My fear is not useful. My regrets, resentments, and holding onto grudges are not helpful.

REALIZE WHAT WOULD BE MORE USEFUL: Perhaps I can learn to be more grateful, or accept my past choices. I can start trusting others and myself more. I can accept that we are just human and forgive others and self.

ANNOUNCE WHAT YOU NO LONGER WANT: I no longer want to fear. It prevents me from taking risks. I no longer want to regret my past; it holds me back. I no longer want to be resentful and unforgiving.

STATE WHAT YOU DO WANT: I do want to become grateful for what I have. I want to have faith in myself, others and God. I want to accept my past mistakes. I want to make better future choices. I want to accept others and myself. I want to forgive myself and others and become a more loving person.

HAUL AWAY WHAT IS NO LONGER USEFUL: As of this day I give up my need to wallow in negativity. I no longer choose to live in fear. I will no longer regret my past. I give up my right to be resentful and unforgiving.

INITIATE A USEFUL REPLACEMENT: This day I will replace negative thoughts with ones of gratitude. I have decided to replace my fear with love for God, others, and self. I will replace my resentment, with understanding, and my regrets, with acceptance. I will forgive myself and others.

TENDER MOMENT: We experience inner peace once we reject what hinders us, accept our past mistakes, forgive others, and embrace what is more useful.

STEP TWO - BECOME GRATEFUL

STOP! THINK!

WHAT ARE YOU GRATEFUL FOR? Is it your health, your family, your friends, your past successes, your appearance, your job, your life style? (When being grateful we do not compare ourselves to others.)

START: Recalling all that we are grateful for in our every thought.

These two steps work because they bring our negative thoughts that harm us to our conscious mind. When that occurs, we can deal with the painful aspects of our lives and do something about them. A change of heart has the power to change our lives. Only our heart can love the unlovable, forgive the unforgivable and accept the unacceptable.

What do you want to trash? What are you grateful for?

                                      ✌ Mary Gale Hinrichsen

Are You Walking Past Your Future?

Ann M. Preston

*E*veryone we meet contributes to who we are. Some may make a greater or more lasting impact but, nonetheless, they all have an effect on us.

When I was in the fifth grade I met a girl in homeroom named MaryAnne. My last name started with a "P" and her last named started with an "R", so she was seated right behind me in our row. Thank goodness there wasn't anyone with a last name that started with a "Q," or I might not have gotten to know my lifelong best friend! We're still "BIFFS" (Best Inseparable Friends Forever) to this day and, although we live in separate parts of the country and our lives are very different, I can't imagine what my future would have been like if I didn't have "Mare" to share all of my hopes and dreams with over the years.

Have you ever met someone and known, immediately, that they would have a huge impact on your life? Think of that person for a moment and try to imagine what life would have been like if you had walked right past, without ever meeting them. Whether it's personal or professional, we never know who will be the next person to alter our future. I believe this so strongly that I started a business based on this concept and called it, "Freedom Builders."

Freedom Builders was founded in September 2001, just one week before the 9/11 tragedy. My intention was to create a business networking environment for people to obtain leads and referrals. But soon, I realized that if we only look for "prospects," then we are really missing out. We quickly adapted the model to teach our members to look for strategic alliances and business resources within the group. Just because someone cannot give you a business lead does not mean they cannot significantly influence the future of your business.

I'll share another wonderful friend with you. You may have heard of Matt Bacak. I met Matt in a bookstore. We had agreed to meet there so he could join Freedom Builders. He quickly became one of our most talked-about members and his business began to skyrocket. One day he told me that he was going to be the author of a best-selling book. Through Matt and his book, I met Lee Beard and Steven E and became involved in the *Wake Up* series. I was even the "cover girl" featured on one of the *Wake Up* magazines. I have also been a guest on many of the Wake Up teleconferences, where I have shared my passion for Freedom Builders. People listening across the country have called to ask how they can start Freedom Builders in their city! At a Wake Up seminar last year in San Diego I met Marilyn Fitch, one of the co-authors of this book. In that chance meeting, Marilyn embraced the Freedom Builders vision and is now the CEO of Freedom Builders San Diego. She has become a great friend and source of tremendous inspiration and wisdom for me. I even call her "Mom."

So you see, if I told Matt to simply "mail me a check" instead of taking the time to meet him and get to know him, Freedom Builders would still be "that little idea" I once had. Instead, it now exists in six major cities in the United States. My mission is to grow Freedom Builders around the world and have this wonderful concept impact and improve as many lives as possible.

I'd like to share with you the greatest lesson I've learned in life so far—and I share it with much gratitude to Mare and everyone I have met along the way. View every person you meet as a great resource. Climb the ladder to success one new friend at a time, in both your personal life and your profession. Most importantly, seize the opportunity to connect with every person you meet. If you walk past, you may just walk past your future.

ಉ Ann Preston

Gratefully Embrace Who You Are

Dr. Nell Rodgers

People loved me. I could feel it. Clients reported miracles. I worked hard and diligently. My bank account was healthy. I ran three miles daily, meditated each morning and chose healthy foods. I traveled the world. My home was a haven. Colleagues, friends and clients respected me. I was outstanding in my field. People traveled from across America to avail themselves of my work. I had it all.

Still, I felt restless, frustrated, and unfulfilled. I loved my clients and felt grateful that they trusted me to mentor their healthcare. By external standards I was living the blessed life, yet deep inside I yearned to be free. Even though I studied harder to learn more and extended myself in service, I felt shackled. I wrote in my journal, repeated affirmations, prayed, meditated, and wept. My mind told me to express gratitude for my blessed life, so each morning I ritualistically gave thanks. Yet, on a deeper level I suppressed myself, refusing to acknowledge my innermost passion. Eventually I became ill, but compelled my body to return to the office, willing myself to continue what I believed to be "right."

When engaged with a client, implementing my skills, I felt terrific. But underneath, the yearning, craving, and angst were ever present. I wanted to walk away. My spiritual quest led to deeper understandings and I began to see that I would never be free until I honored and appreciated my heart-song. Teaching, singing and acting are my first love and would have been my career choice had my father permitted it. In the presence of abundance I had become a victim; doing the "right thing;" stuck in languishing for what might have been instead of praising and appreciating my passion. My misery and attachment kept me from moving and lack of movement made me miserable. While I expressed joy, positivity, a hopeful outlook and felicity to my clients and friends, I was heartsick.

To feed my hungry spirit, I took acting lessons. As impossible as it may seem, I won a role with every audition. On stage, I felt vivacious and passionate. But, how could I leave a thriving practice, a handsome income, a life of prestige? How could I desert the clients

I loved, who depended upon me, who loved me? How could I cast off this "optimal" life and step into nothing? I was unwilling to walk away until sheer fatigue and weariness from internal conflict forced me to sell my practice.

I was free! I was still respected, loved and revered. I had time to sing, write, and be on stage.

The support from my friends, colleagues and clients was amazing. They honored that I had found the courage to walk away. Some took my lead and left jobs in which they were miserable.

Without fail, each of us has been rewarded for our willingness to honor the fire within; to create a life which is aligned with inner spirit and passion; to appreciate ourselves. Each day I feel grateful for my courage.

Life changes are not always easy and others may not support you. Some will think you are crazy or question your motives. Ignorance is continuing to believe the same thing in the presence of knowledge. Craziness is staying in a situation which drains energy, squelches desire, blots out creativity and sucks away life. Sanity comes with integrity, personal fulfillment, a commitment to soul longings and deep appreciation of who you are.

Lack of self-approval and failure to be grateful promotes agony. Be willing to love yourself enough to shed your misery. Be grateful for who you are. The personal work of altering deep-seated beliefs may be tedious or intense and rewards may not be immediately obvious.

However, valuing your talents, appreciating your abilities and honoring your passion will free you to explore and become all that you desire to be. Your soul will be nurtured. Gratitude will fill your heart.

I have established a situation which allows me to see clients if I wish, or see no one; something everyone thought impossible. No longer a victim of circumstance, I travel the world. I still serve humanity. The difference is that my spirit is thriving and I am doing what I love. I still make mistakes but I am alive! Each day I give thanks for all that I have and for all that I am.

၁ Dr Nell Rodgers

Problems as Opportunities
Denise Yamada

One of my favorite quotations is from Maya Angelou: "The need for change bulldozed a road down the center of my mind."

In January of 2001, the need for change bulldozed its way through the middle of my life! After what I thought were six happy years of employment as the main news anchor at one of the top television stations in San Diego, California, my contract was not renewed. Enter the bulldozer. I was completely flattened. I was sad and afraid. I felt lost because the job that had defined me for 23 years was over.

There was a grieving process I had to go through before I could realize that this loss was actually a **gift**. For four months, I did whatever I wanted—even if that meant doing nothing at all. I spent countless hours lying in front of a blazing fire, watching the flames devour my old way of being and doing life. I savored the colors of the sunset and delighted in the way the eucalyptus trees in my backyard danced in the wind. I took long walks with no particular destination other than to the center of myself. It was life at its simplest and life at its best.

I could have taken another television job. Instead, I chose self-imposed exile. After 23 years of public service and life in the limelight, I needed a break. My job had been to tell people what was broken, bad, and wrong in the world and who was to blame for it. More than two decades of that as my main diet left me depressed, demoralized, and defeated. No wonder my contract wasn't renewed. I realized that it was actually ***perfect*** that I was unemployed because I'd outgrown that old life and could no longer live that way. I had been unwilling to shed that life, but that was exactly what was necessary for me to create a new life.

When I took stock of my television career, there were highlights, of course. I'd earned seven Emmy© awards for my work. They had all been for stories about love, faith, courage, and community. Those stories were about the good that lies in each of us and all around us. They weren't stories that left people dispirited and heartbroken. Rather, they were stories that brought people together and empowered them to go out and transform a corner of their world, a life in their community.

So this is where and how I began to build my new life. I started by being grateful. It all boiled down to asking myself this question: "What is this problem an opportunity for?" Trust me; it wasn't that eloquent in the beginning. It was more like looking for the proverbial silver lining in the dark cloud. And it worked. By doing this simple thing, I actually **created** a new experience of life. Instead of this event being something destructive, it became an opportunity for growth.

Everybody has problems. Life is a series of people, events, and circumstances that comes into our lives—so often disguised as "problems." But problems aren't really the issue. It's how we deal with them. What usually happens when we encounter problems? We get stuck, depressed, or angry. Or we become unfocused, helpless, and defeated. Have you noticed how things have a tendency to spiral downward from there?

What would be possible if you were to expand the way you think about problems? Close your eyes for a minute and think about how you feel when you hear "If it's not one thing, it's another." Or "What can go wrong **will** go wrong." They make you feel deflated and kind of yucky, don't they? Now close your eyes and see how you feel when you hear *"For what is this an opportunity?"* It's like a door opening, or an invitation, isn't it?

I took it as an invitation to explore a new line of work—one that empowers people to live life by design, not default. I am now a certified professional life coach. I am so grateful for the years I spent in television news reporting all the stories, good and bad, and for all the marvelous people with whom I've had the privilege to work and interview. When I walked out of the television station that night in January of 2001, I couldn't begin to imagine how I'd make anything of all I'd been through and all I'd been given. Gratefully, I realize who I am: Not just a writer or broadcaster or mother or life coach, but someone who can use every gift I've been given in the service of others.

                           ల Denise Yamada

Journey to Paradise
Thu-Anh Hoang, M.D.

I was born in South Vietnam to an army physician father and a housewife mother during the war.

I wanted to be a doctor since I was 8 years old, after reading about Albert Schweitzer's work as a physician in Africa. I grew up speaking both Vietnamese and French. English was my third language. I always dreamed of studying medicine in the United States although I knew it was nearly impossible for a non-citizen to attend U.S. medical schools—not to mention the prohibitive cost. Nevertheless, I studied and took all the necessary tests as if I was going to go to college in the United States.

I left Vietnam on October 16, 1974, to attend the University of Paris VI Faculty of Sciences. I was to major in Life Sciences. I lost my former country on April 30, 1975, during the Communist take over, and my parents fled on a South Vietnamese Navy boat and were picked up by the US Navy in the South China Sea.

An orthopedic surgeon in Mason City, Iowa, helped organize a refresher course for Vietnamese physicians at the University of Iowa in Iowa City. Several churches in town sponsored three Vietnamese physicians (one of whom was my father) to resettle in Mason City. Living in Paris, I had been accepted to enter medical school in the fall of 1975. I decided to throw out my opportunity to become a physician in France to realize my dream of becoming one in the United States, inspired by what my father had to do to be able to practice medicine again in the U.S.

I had the biggest culture shock of my life, moving from cosmopolitan Paris to Mason City, with its population of 40,000 in 1975. I had a headache for six months trying to read people's lips since I had studied British English. I tested out of my first college English course and was placed in the second semester English class during my first semester at the University of Iowa. The teacher gave me a B+ which infuriated me since I had earned A's in all the other subjects. I did not want any more B's in classes that had essays on which could be rated subjectively. I changed my major from Premed to Biomedical

Engineering since I excelled in Math and Physics. I graduated Magna Cum Laude and went on to medical school.

For many years of sitting on the fence between the two cultures, I didn't feel I belonged to either. I felt too Americanized for my Vietnamese compatriots and still too Vietnamese for my American counterparts. I picked the best of each culture to build my own life in which I marched to the sound of my own drums and did what I felt was right for the circumstances. It has now been thirty years since I have arrived in the U.S. I have been a U.S. citizen for 22 years. On November 2, 2004, after voting in the presidential election, my soul finally felt more American than Vietnamese.

I am very grateful and proud to be a US citizen. Why?

1- This is the ultimate land of opportunity. This is the only country in the world where anyone can realize her dreams if she is willing to work hard, be patient and persistent. This is the Promised Land.

2- Southern California is Paradise on Earth. The climate is warm and sunny most of the time. The most authentic and delicious Vietnamese cuisine is being served in Little Saigon (Westminster). People are very friendly and smile often (even acquaintances from out of state notice that).

3- The US is the ultimate "melting pot" for many ethnic populations. California is the "international state" and Los Angeles, where I live, is probably the most cosmopolitan and ethnically is, at least as, diverse as New York City. What an opportunity for learning about other cultures while savoring their delectable cuisines!

4- I am thankful for all the wonderful opportunities my new country has given me to become a neuroradiologist (radiologist specializing in diseases of the brain, spine, head and neck), and to meet all the people from many nations who are my neighbors, colleagues and patients. I am also thankful to have attended a "Wake Up Succeed" seminar in my quest to find serenity, inner peace, and realize my professional potential. The people I met at the seminar happen to be the teachers who appear now that the student is ready.

I vow to serve my countrymen, American and Vietnamese, to the best of my ability, under the guidance of God, my newly-rediscovered old friend.

ख Thu-Anh Hoang, M.D.

The Angel Purred
Kathleen Hudson

*L*ife is a celebration. I found that out when I became the final companion to a dying parent. Those precious last six months will hold me in an attitude of gratitude for life. I can breathe freely, I have my health, and I have lasting, sustaining memories shared in love and laughter. Memories are a wonderful blessing on this earth. We can make more memories, recall those in the past, and get very creative in spending time together and alone. The mind chooses to use distraction when pain is present or when it makes the choice to be in denial of any event.

For the first year of Mom's disease, there were only minor changes in her life. The last year was full of daily challenges, surprises, and events that were part of the process. Each day is a gift from God; we call it the present and it is ours to make whatever we want. Some days are better than others; some are worse. In pain management, you have both good days and bad days.

New adventures in the life of a dying person can be likened to the wide-eyed view a baby takes when seeing something for the first time. The views are more special, as they have to last. They are crisper in nature; they have a bond to reality that is more special, precious, and endearing. The mind thinks and remembers in pictures. The mind moves back and forth in the timeline of life, touching places it remembers and anchoring thoughts to moments of pleasure and pain. Our emotions guide our reactions to those memories. Mom had days that were a whirlwind of emotion. She remembered times of remorse, shame, and guilt. She would get stuck in a negative memory and tough out the wave of emotion she was feeling. My comment, "It's not happening to you now," would snap her back into the present and give her peace. Some days just listening was enough. Some days I had to rely on the Holy Spirit for guidance. The walk as a final companion requires much prayer.

I was amazed at the triggers that would set off a time of release. Lisa was a volunteer caregiver who had a lot of cats and one kitten. One evening, Lisa asked me if I thought mom would enjoy playing with the kitten. Mom was an animal lover. I remember growing up with a dog and a cat that were very attached to mom. Buddy and Puddin Tat were quite old when I returned from college in 1970, and when mom and dad moved to Arizona in 1976, the critters were put to sleep. Mom always felt bad about not taking the pets with her, even though she knew they probably wouldn't have survived the flight. I told Lisa that mom would enjoy playing with the kitten.

Lisa's kitten was a fur ball of energy about seven weeks old and very tiny. She was black and tan with a small circle of white on her head between her ears, as if someone had painted a halo on her. Mom called her "Angel Kitty." Those few hours brought back a flood of memories of pets from the past. There was the dog my father smuggled home from Germany after WWII; Sputnik was his name. There was a sheep dog mix that followed mom home from work one day; his name was Chummy.

Brownie was the first dog we picked out from the SPCA; he hated kids. She remembered that he bit the neighbor's boy and how I cried when he disappeared. About two weeks later we got Buddy. He was a part of the family for 12 years. He loved beer and boating. Once he fell in the Niagara River and had to swim for about 20 minutes until some fishermen rescued him. Buddy created adventures and mom remembered them all. She reminded me how much Buddy despised Puddin when I brought her home but he tolerated her in his house.

"Angel Kitty" brought a time to reflect and heal over animals from the past.

She was just the right medicine for mom. Healing comes in many forms. Touching the soft warm fur and hearing the purr of a small kitten, can be a portal to memories. This was a very pleasurable experience for mom. She was so involved that she forgot her physical pain for a few hours. She thanked Lisa for bringing "Angel Kitty" for a visit.

The Bible tells us that we may meet Angels unaware, that they can grace us with their presence at anytime. In my prayer time during the last days of mom's life, I could feel the presence of angels. I am grateful for the time we shared. Though it was often difficult, it was one of the most rewarding times of my life.

ペ Kathleen Hudson

In Due Season

Dr. Linda Owens

*L*ife doesn't care what you are, but who you are. I am in the business of changing people's lives.

In 1999, my divorce was final. I was devastated. I had a home with a mortgage, a car note, two small children, and a new consulting business—all of which were creating countless bills. How was I going to make it? I was on Atlanta's #1 radio station giving relationship advice of all things. What would happen to my credibility? How would I handle the guilt and shame of being divorced and a single mom?

I was entering a season of life that I now refer to as my "season of seeking." I was hurt, lonely, and confused. I lacked direction. Nothing in life had meaning. At that time, I was seeking to find out who I was. I had to redefine myself. I was no longer a wife, no longer a self-assured and confident woman. I was no longer on top of my game personally or professionally. I was searching for answers to the questions "Why?" "How?" "Now what?"

In his infinite wisdom, God stepped in and showed me that seeking is not always a bad thing. When people seek, we assume that they are uncertain or lacking direction. If you are the seeker, you often feel anxious and insecure. When you are seeking, it is a time to ask questions; to discover who you are and whose you are. It helps you to identify your strengths and your weaknesses. Everything you have began with a search. For example, you may have sought a job, a house, a car, a relationship. Sometimes in life, we seek the wrong thing or we seek the right thing but at the wrong time. Seeking is not necessarily a bad thing, for it is in seeking that you find. The key is to discover *what* you are seeking.

As I focused my search, I found my purpose and entered another season: the "season of securing." Once you find your purpose, you need to develop yourself to walk in it. This requires reading and listening to audio tapes to help you develop a positive mind. Joyce Myers said, "You cannot have a positive life with a negative mind." You must go through a period of transformation. If you want to have things you've never had before you must do things you've never done before. It involves surrounding yourself with people of similar vision and purpose. Your network will determine your net worth. You need a good mentor and a good life coach. Find a good life coach who will help you set goals, help you develop a strategic plan, help you identify resources, hold you accountable, and perhaps, most importantly, help you celebrate your successes. Just as iron sharpens iron, so man sharpens man. And through it all, do not forget to pray.

Once you step into the realization of who you are, whose you are, and the abundance that goes along with it, it is up to you to lock down that which belongs to you. Secure it and make it your own. Then you will develop a whole new level of confidence. Your smile, your posture, your walk, is different. You will have been transformed. Every aspect of your being will exude success. You will be in the "season of soaring."

". . . but those who hope in the Lord will renew their strength. They will soar on wings like eagles; they will run and not grow weary, they will walk and not be faint."   *Isaiah 40:31 NIV*

I have done my seeking. I have done my securing. And now, praise be to God, I am soaring! I attribute much of my success to the trials and tribulations in my life. I am grateful for them, for without the test, there can be no testimony. It has been said, "Things may happen around you and things may happen to you, but the only things that count are the things that happen in you." I am grateful for the changes within me, and for all of my seasons. Through my seasons of seeking, securing, and soaring, I found my purpose and my passion. I have developed a plan—and it works! I have more time for my children and they are flourishing. I have expanded my business. In addition to corporate training and consulting, we now do professional development and life coaching. I do motivational and keynote speaking on a variety of topics, and I host an internet-based radio talk show designed to help people maximize their potential while finding balance in their lives. I have learned a strategy for living a happier, healthier, more flexible lifestyle. Now, it is my mission to share my strategy with you. Imagine stepping out of who you are and stepping into who you can become!

"There is a time for everything and a season for every activity under heaven," (*Ecclesiastes 3:1 NIV*). What season are you in? Are you searching for answers? Are you redefining yourself? Are you taking the opportunity to gratefully seize every opportunity that comes to you? Are you growing stronger with each life lesson? Perhaps this is your season to soar. Whatever your season, recognize that you are there by divine appointment. Get all that you can from the "gift" of your season. Gratitude does not result from receiving the gift, but from the application of the gift in your life.

And it all occurs in due season.

℘ Dr. Linda Owens

Talk With My Dad
Lee Beard

I have heard that gratitude and love are two of the most powerful words in the world. I believe it.

I can't think of gratitude without thinking about my family. I didn't realize what a good home life I had growing up until I went to college and found that most people there didn't like going home on the weekends. I enjoyed going home. Many students can't wait to go to college to get away from home. The main thing I noticed about being away from home at college was that, should I have car trouble or for any other reason get stranded and fail to come in at night, no one was going to come looking for me.

I can remember being glad that someone came looking for me one day when I left my horse to go hunting in the woods, and he went back to the barn without me. I got involved with a hunt with several of our dogs and neglected my horse. I could tell that he tried to follow us for awhile but obviously decided that we had deserted him. So, he started home. When the horse arrived without me, my father got in his truck and came looking for me. I had started walking home and a truck driver picked me up when I saw my dad.

I consider myself most fortunate to have been raised in the home that I did. I've heard that you can't pick your parents; however, I could not have picked a better pair. I realize now that I can't remember hearing a harsh word from my parents toward each other or the children. I was the middle child of five and, even with the obvious older brother and older sister rivalries, we have had a life long experience of trust and happiness together.

The foundation for my life and business came from my family and I seem to remember more of what my father told me as I go though life. My faith in God came from my parents, who took me to church throughout my childhood. The friends that I met in church and in related activities were a major influence at that time and are still today.

I'm reminded often of the wisdom that my father gave me when I asked him for advice. His words were "Everybody's got to make his own mistakes." I told him then that it wasn't any help. But the more

I'm around this world and involved in life with wife, children and business the truer his words become.

The other thing that I got from my father was the desire to be free. When we worked on the farm, I've told people that the only day that was different was Sunday. All other days were work days. Yet, as hard as he labored, I had a sense from my father that he never went to work because farming was his love. If he had never gone 20 miles from his home, he would have been happy. I believe that I got my desire "not to work" from him. So, I'm grateful that I saw freedom in my father's business life and that I was not born lazy.

I'm reminded of my first network television show experience which was with the popular country music show, "Hee Haw." The image always depicted on that show was of lazy farm days with lazy people and lazy dogs on the front porch. Contrary to that image of southern farm life, I don't remember a lot of sitting around. Im fact, my son commented after one visit to the farm that we were unusual people because, after dinner, we would go out and pick up pecans instead of lounging around. I never have been good at just sitting still.

As I write, it becomes apparent that gratitude and love go together. I'm grateful for the love that I knew from my home life. Also, gratitude is like love. You can give it away and keeping giving it away and you will never run out of it. You'll never deplete your supply, and "what goes around, comes around."

So spread it on thick.

ϛ Lee Beard

Author Index

Sharyn is the CEO and founder of Elite Leads Business Development, founder of Speakers Collaborative, author of *Mixing It Up! The Entrepreneur's New Testament, Making a List and Checking it Twice! What Singles Need to Know, J.O.B.S. Just Over Broke Syndrome, Street Smart Sales: Personality Recognition, Your Right to Write,* and *Speak Easy.* Sharyn is a motivational speaker who inspires her audiences to live the life of their dreams, now! She is available for trainings, seminars, and corporate events and keynotes. Contact her at:
(925) 939-1801
www.eliteleads.com
www.sharynabbott.com
Sharyn@eliteleads.com

Michael is the President of a successful Real Estate Acquisition Company in Mississippi, where he has bought, sold, and managed millions of dollars worth of real estate properties. To discover how to become wealthy using real estate as a vehicle, enroll in a free course at: www.FreeREITraining.com To contact him directly, call 601-948-5445
e-mail to: MichaelAdulAli@gmail.com

Eileen Ashmore works with individuals and businesses to assist them in building business and marketing strategies for their next level of development. Eileen has an MBA in Marketing and over the last 19 years has worked on over 160 projects with client businesses. Visit Eileen's website at www.ashmore-assoc.com for marketing ideas and more information on the 25+ marketing strategies available to assist you and your company to become more successful.

Victoria is working on a collection of stories about overcoming barriers to success and happiness. "If you are interested in sharing about how you plan to or have transformed your life, triumphed over obstacles and adversity, please email your testimonial or story to BeforetheButterfly@yahoo.com." Contact her: c/o Penelope Alleyne, Senior Vice President & Public Relations 2900 NW 47th Terrace
Lauderdale Lakes, FL 33313
803-270-3087

A former television producer and business developer, Lee lives in Arkansas when not traveling as co-creator of the Wake Up book series. An author featured in more than a dozen motivational and inspirational volumes, he concentrates on bringing the power of the Wake Up network to bear on the challenges of business development. You may contact him at: lee@wakeuplive.com.

For your free gift, go to: **www.wakeupand.com**

Wake up... Live the Life You Love, Giving Gratitude

For your free gift, go to: **www.wakeupand.com**

www.waynedyer.com
Best-selling author and lecturer
Author of the best-seller *Power of Intention, Real Magic, Manifesting Your Destiny, and Pulling Your Own Strings.*

Charleen is a freelance writer for the *San Francisco Chronicle, Stockton Record, Diablo Magazine, Brentwood Press, Antioch Press, Good News* (Northern California's only Christian newspaper), and more. Her beats include: features, human interest, sports-features, entertainment, and humor columns. She's a stand-up comedienne who performs throughout the United States; under the stage name of "Charlie B. Earley." She co-produces an annual comedy show called, "Comedy Night at the Village," to benefit the National Ovarian Cancer Coalition. She's author of *Funny Side Up*, a compilation of over 70 published humor columns, and founder of the **LOT** (**L**east **O**f **T**hese) Foundation. When she's not speaking, writing, or playing comedy clubs, she's with her son riding their two Arabian horses in Stockton, CA. Contact her at: charleno@ecis.com Website: www.CharleenEarley.com Phone: (925) 383-3072

Marilyn is the CEO of Freedom Builders San Diego. "Together we can share the vision of connecting businesses with each other so that we may all improve and become more successful as we build out networking community." You can contact her at:
619-647-9996
Website: www.freedombuilderssandiego.com
E-mail at: marilyn@freedombuilderssandiego.com

Evani Collections
phone: 310-675-3560
fax: 310-675-3081
www.evanicollections.com

Natural Approaches to Radiant Health
(310) 445-3350
ENerQi@sbcglobal.net
www.GraysonAcupunture.com

Wake up... Live the Life You Love, Giving Gratitude

For your free gift, go to: **www.wakeupand.com**

Dr. Linda Owens is in the business of changing people's lives. She is an author, motivational speaker, trainer, and life coach. Her radio show "Ask Dr. Linda" can be heard around the world through her website www.drlindaowens. com. Dr. Owens is best known for her work in the area of effective relationships, both at home and in diverse workplace environments. Contact her at: The Owens Group, Inc.
Website: www.drlindaowens.com
E-mail Linda at: linda@drlindaowens.com
Phone: 1-877-DROWENS (376-9367)

Mind Mastery Coaching
Speaker, Life Strategist
(818) 972-4415
Hazel@MindMasteryCoaching.com
www.MindMasterycoaching.com

A speaker and trainer, Cappi brings a background in corporate sales and real estate to the task of coaching and consulting her clients from her base in Irvine, California. It is when people are in a state of change that Cappi can help the most as a Transformation Consultant. Contact here at: 770 Irvine Center Drive, Suite 800, Irvine, CA 92618.
Phone: 949-753-2865
E-mail: cappi@CappiPidwell.com

Catherine "Kay" Presto broke the gender barrier for journalists covering NASCAR, and was named the 2005 "Woman of Achievement" by the National Association for Female Executives (NAFE). An aggressive entrepreneur, she invites everyone to send a Sensational Senior story to: Presto Productions, 1711 N. Leeds Avenue, Ontario, CA 91764
Phone & Fax: 909-985-3041
E-mail: prestoprod@juno.com

Ann Preston is the Founder & CEO of Freedom Builders, the fastest growing business networking system in the world. Ann has been featured on national TV, broadcast on live interviews nationwide, featured on magazine covers and spoken at countless events with world class speakers like Mike Victor Hansen, Blair Singer, Tom Antion and Stedman Graham. As a Visioneer, Ann is aggressively pursuing the international growth of the Freedom Builders Business Networking System.
Visit the Freedom Builders website at: www.FreedomBuildersInc.com
Contact Ann by e-mail at: Ann@FreedomBuildersInc.com
or by phone at: 770-452-3324

A Certified Professional Life Coach, Award-Winning Journalist and Keynote Speaker, Denise brings years of communication experience to her work with others. You may contact her at:
Denise Yamada Coaching
P.O. Box 90459
San Diego, CA 92169
619-948-3904
denise@dyamada.com
www.deniseyamada.com

John, a former draughtsman and designer emigrated to Canada in 1966 with his first wife, Kay. He was a sailing instructor in Vancouver, and later a power line designer in Calgary. "People wonder about RNVR," he says, "and I was in the Royal Navy Reserve, but to me it means, "REVITALIZED! NOT VERY RETIRED, REARING TO GO." Contact John at cjohnyeo@shaw.ca.

Brian Yui co-founded HouseRebate.com in 1999. Utilizing 15 years of real estate experience, he created a full-service online/offline real estate broker-age firm. Prior to obtaining his real estate broker's license, Brian spent five years at Price Waterhouse Coopers as a Certified Public Accountant. He holds a M.B.T. degree from the University of Southern California and a B.S. degree from the University of California, Berkley. In his spare time, Brian enjoys traveling, kayaking, cooking, yoga and being involved in charity work. Contact him at: brian@houserebate.com
Website: www.houserebate.com